Priorities for
Academic Libraries

Thomas J. Galvin, Beverly P. Lynch, *Editors*

NEW DIRECTIONS FOR HIGHER EDUCATION

MARTIN KRAMER, *Editor-in-Chief*

Number 39, September 1982

Paperback sourcebooks in
The Jossey-Bass Higher Education Series

Jossey-Bass Inc., Publishers
San Francisco • Washington • London

Priorties for Academic Libraries
Volume X, Number 3, September 1982
Thomas J. Galvin, Beverly P. Lynch, *Editors*

New Directions for Higher Education Series
Martin Kramer, *Editor-in-Chief*

New Directions for Higher Education (publication number USPS
990-880) is published quarterly by Jossey-Bass Inc., Publishers.
New Directions is numbered sequentially — please order extra
copies by sequential number. The volume and issue numbers
above are included for the convenience of libraries. Second-class
postage rates paid at San Francisco, California, and at
additional mailing offices.

Correspondence:
Subscriptions, single-issue orders, change of address notices,
undelivered copies, and other correspondence should be sent to
New Directions Subscriptions, Jossey-Bass Inc., Publishers,
433 California Street, San Francisco, California 94104.

Editorial correspondence should be sent to the Consulting Editor,
Martin Kramer, 2807 Shasta Road, Berkeley, California 94708.

Library of Congress Catalogue Card Number LC 81-48572
International Standard Serial Number ISSN 0271-0560
International Standard Book Number ISBN 87589-897-1

Cover art by Willi Baum
Manufactured in the United States of America

Ordering Information

The paperback sourcebooks listed below are published quarterly and can be ordered either by subscription or as single copies.

Subscriptions cost $35.00 per year for institutions, agencies, and libraries. Individuals can subscribe at the special rate of $21.00 per year *if payment is by personal check.* (Note that the full rate of $35.00 applies if payment is by institutional check, even if the subscription is designated for an individual.) Standing orders are accepted.

Single copies are available at $7.95 when payment accompanies order, and *all single-copy orders under $25.00 must include payment.* (California, Washington, D.C., New Jersey, and New York residents please include appropriate sales tax.) For billed orders, cost per copy is $7.95 plus postage and handling. (Prices subject to change without notice.)

To ensure correct and prompt delivery, all orders must give either the *name of an individual* or an *official purchase order number.* Please submit your order as follows:

Subscriptions: specify series and subscription year.
Single Copies: specify sourcebook code and issue number (such as, HE8).

Mail orders for United States and Possessions, Latin America, Canada, Japan, Australia, and New Zealand to:
    Jossey-Bass Inc., Publishers
    433 California Street
    San Francisco, California 94104

Mail orders for all other parts of the world to:
    Jossey-Bass Limited
    28 Banner Street
    London EC1Y 8QE

New Directions for Higher Education Series
Martin Kramer, *Editor-in-Chief*

Contents

Editor's Notes

University and college librarians historically have complained that their libraries were the victims of benign neglect by academic administrators. For better or worse, that classic syndrome appears, of late, to be reversing itself. The academic library now is a prime focus of administrative attention on many campuses. And, if not exactly malevolent, that attention seems not always entirely friendly, at least from the librarian's perspective.

The library is one of the largest single cost centers in the institution. Unlike other major cost centers, the library typically has little revenue-generating capacity. It is also one of a small number of units, like food service and parking, about which nearly everybody on the campus considers himself or herself an expert. From senior administrator to professor to lowliest freshman, everyone has an opinion about the quality of library collections and services and has no hesitation in making that opinion public. In summary, the academic library is at once highly visible and highly vulnerable.

It is also complex, occasionally frustrating, and often baffling from the point of view of central administration. The library consumes resources at a prodigious rate, yet despite the best efforts of presidents and fiscal officers to satisfy its seemingly insatiable appetite for dollars, the results satisfy no one — neither students nor faculty nor the librarians themselves. No matter how much money might be earmarked for the library, it is not clear that it would ever be enough. Even the most dedicated university library director responds with a modicum of sympathy to the harrassed academic vice-president who, more than two decades ago, characterized the university library as "a bottomless pit."

Yet everyone understands that we cannot simply throw up our hands in despair and leave the library to sink or swim. Given the unresolvable conflict between infinite demands for library materials and services on the one hand and finite resources on the other, the library must nonetheless be nurtured, sustained, and supported. There simply is no alternative, for without the library there is no university.

But it is not merely support, it is informed support that is needed from central administration. As Robert M. O'Neil makes clear in the opening chapter of this sourcebook, it is not enough for the university administrator merely to love the library; he or she must take the time and make the serious effort that is required to understand the library in all of its splendid complexity. The goal of this sourcebook is to serve as a briefing for those administrators who must come to terms with the library as a central aspect of the academic enterprise.

In Chapter Two, William A. Moffett provides a counterpoint to O'Neil, suggesting a variety of practical means by which library directors and senior administrators can achieve a common understanding of common problems. Chapter Three, by Russell Shank, presents the viewpoint of yet a third group of highly concerned parties — faculty and students.

Chapters Four through Eight, each written by a broadly experienced academic librarian, address five issues that are central, and seem likely to remain central, to the college and university library now and over the next decade. In a chapter that, in our view, might appropriately command the attention of both campus administrators and those concerned with institutional accreditation, Richard J. Talbot offers a penetrating analysis of the "fair share" concept in library funding, along with an assessment of the fiscal implications, both immediate and long term, of library automation. In Chapter Five, Charles B. Osburn reviews current trends in the development of library collections in relation to the conduct of scholarship.

Faced with astronomical and seemingly uncontrollable increases in the cost of books and journals, many librarians and university administrators have looked for financial relief to interinstitutional sharing of library resources, using the mechanism of linking libraries together in networks and consortia. In Chapter Six, Ward Shaw, executive director of just such a network of academic and research libraries, offers a balanced assessment of both the actual costs and the potential benefits of resource sharing. Chapter Five, by Patricia Battin, addresses yet another urgent problem, that of preserving the nation's printed cultural and intellectual heritage, a crisis of enormous magnitude that has not yet engaged the attention of more than a handful of librarians or university administrators.

Libraries, as Talbot points out in discussing their financing, are traditionally highly labor-intensive organizations. Given the fact that 60 percent or more of the annual budget of a typical college or university library goes for staff salaries, it will not be surprising that the longest chapter in this volume, Chapter Eight, is devoted to library personnel. Millicent D. Abell and Jacqueline M. Coolman examine a variety of issues relating to improved use of the library's human resources, many of which require for their resolution the understanding and active support of central administration.

In Chapter Nine, Robert A. Plane, president of Clarkson College, whose controversial new Schuler Educational Resources Center captured national media attention at the time of its opening, offers a philosophical and practical framework for coming to terms with new information technology in a future that is already upon us. As Plane observes, the final step in the college library's evolution occurs when the library is no longer viewed as a place, but instead is considered as a service.

The nine chapters that comprise the core of this sourcebook were all prepared specifically for it. The authors, especially those who are librarians, were asked to write not for their professional colleagues but for an audience of senior academic administrators: university presidents, provosts, and academic and fiscal vice-presidents. The issues that are identified here, while in some instances highly technical, are all ultimately questions of educational and institutional policy that must engage the attention of senior administrators if they are to be successfully addressed and resolved. They are summarized in a concluding section, which also offers a selected bibliography for further reading.

The problems of the academic library will not go away. And they are too large and too important to be ignored or put aside. We and our fellow authors hope that this sourcebook will help academic administrators to find useful and productive ways of thinking about the library in relation to the institution as a whole, both now and in the future.

Thomas J. Galvin
Beverly P. Lynch
Editors

Thomas J. Galvin is dean of the School of Library and Information Science, University of Pittsburgh.

Beverly P. Lynch is university librarian, University of Illinois at Chicago.

The academic library presents a complex challenge
facing both general university administrators and
library directors in this period of rapid change.

The University Administrator's View of the University Library

Robert M. O'Neil

It is the center of research and a key to a university's scholarly distinction. It is a mounting and at times uncontrollable drain on the university's budget. It is a window to the community—both the academic community and the general citizenry. It is the most dependable link with other institutions of higher learning. It can be an administrative headache and at times a battleground of personnel policies. It is the source of greatest promise and greatest problems in the use of new technologies. It is the key to development of new academic programs and the strength of existing programs. It is all of these elements and many more. The university library is, in short, a source of pride and a source of problems. Like the heart in the human body, it is the most vital organ in the academic community, yet it is one that demands special care and understanding to ensure its health and longevity.

No two university administrators would view the university library in precisely the same way. Differences would reflect at the very least the different disciplines from which we come and which, therefore, shape our own perceptions of the libraries that meet our own scholarly needs. For example, administrators who come from faculties of professional schools with specialized branch libraries are likely to have perceptions quite different from those from the arts and sciences who look to the collections of the main university library. And

T. Galvin, B. Lynch (Eds.)., *New Directions for Higher Education: Priorities for Academic Libraries*, no. 39.
San Francisco: Jossey-Bass, September 1982.

those administrators who come from primarily nonacademic backgrounds are likely to see the university library in yet different ways, if perhaps more objectively than those of us whose backgrounds are primarily academic and thus bring to administrative office many years of close contact with research library collections.

Any attempt, therefore, to distill "the university administrator's" view of the university library involves individuals and perspectives from too broad and diverse a group to permit easy assimilation. Let us begin with several assumptions about the environment facing university libraries in the next decade or so.

First, the costs of library materials will continue to increase at a rate in excess of the rise in the consumer price index. (In several recent years, the ratio of costs of library materials to the general inflationary index has, of course, been almost two to one and, for certain highly specialized publications — medical journals, for example — it has substantially exceeded even this ratio.) Any administrator who does not anticipate such continuing and overscale cost increases is simply not looking realistically at recent experience and probable extrapolation from it.

Second, both the availability of and the need for new technologies will continue to inflate university library costs. Not only in cataloging and circulation, but also in bibliographic systems and other areas, the availability of new technologies and the broader acceptance of them by the major university libraries will surely make such new (and costly) systems a virtual necessity for other research libraries as well.

Third, external funding (both from governmental and private sources) cannot possibly meet the special and growing needs of university libraries. Whatever happens to such federal programs as the very welcome support for research libraries under Title II C of the Higher Education Act of 1965, major governmental subvention cannot be assumed as a significant source of relief. Nor can the major foundations be expected to offset substantially the major institutional needs and expenses. Some external support (both public and private) will undoubtedly continue to exist; dependence upon it should, however, be viewed as marginal rather than as central.

Fourth, limits on interinstitutional cooperation and resource sharing must realistically be recognized and accepted. Although some progress has been made toward better collaboration and sharing of materials, and more can be done in the future with improved informational tools, there are unavoidable limits beyond which complimentary collection development may not proceed.

Fifth, and on a more hopeful note, storage of seldom-used materials is likely to become much more efficient and the space required for such storage less urgent than it may once have appeared. Not only the increasing use of microforms and more efficient shelving, but also more systematic weeding of existing collections, may reduce the need for major new facilities for overflow. Moreover, in this area, interinstitutional resource sharing — as reflected, for example, in the Center for Research Libraries — presumably has its greatest potential.

These five desiderata should at least set the stage. They do not offer an altogether reassuring prospect for the 1980s and 1990s. Yet they do at least describe the challenge that faces general university administrators and library directors in a period of rapid change. Against this background, we might now explore two sets of issues — one at the local or institutional level and the other at the national level. As the university administrator views the library, he or she naturally considers several specific contexts in which the library plays a special role.

Issues on Campus

1. *Academic program development and review.* It is always jarring to discover a procedure for approving new academic degree programs that does not require an assessment of impact upon the library and library collections. A conscientious academic administrator will, in fact, insist upon such an appraisal — presumably by the library director or the subject or area specialist — before approving a proposed degree, whatever may be its other merits. To institute a new program without adequate library support — or without having made provision for supplemental materials sufficient to the discipline — is either to jeopardize the program or to place the library (after the fact) in an impossible position.

Such an objective can be accomplished in several ways. The format for degree review and approval may simply contain a section for the assessment of library resources — both existing collections and additions needed to serve the proposed program. Or an appropriate member of the library professional staff (conceivably the dean or director) could serve as a member of the faculty review committee and thus participate directly in discussions on the degree program. Either method — or some combination of the two — should serve the essential purpose of library involvement in assessing the university's capacity to mount and sustain new degree programs in times of scarce resources.

Even the recruitment of a new faculty member with a novel specialty may cause comparable problems. Although it is obviously not possible to obtain library approval each time faculty recruitment expands the department's disciplinary horizons and its bibliographic needs, informal consultation before an offer is made may help to avoid grief later, for both the library staff and the recruit.

2. *The faculty committee and library policies.* Few relationships in a university are more delicate than those between the teaching faculty and the profes-

sional library staff. The focus of this relationship is usually an elected or appointed faculty advisory committee. It is with that committee that the library director and senior staff members must work closely if they are to gain and maintain essential broad support from the faculty at large. Several measures may facilitate cooperation. The library director should be consulted regarding nominations or appointments to the library committee. Some effort should be made to ensure continuity in the faculty membership. The head of the committee should be particularly sympathetic toward and well versed in university library policies and operations. Perhaps most important, the respective roles of committee and librarians should be clearly defined, making clear that, while the faculty committee advises on overall policy and direction, it is the director and staff who must make the day-to-day operating decisions if the library is to function effectively. (At times, particular policies—those involving recall of materials borrowed by the faculty, the use of studies and carrels, and other policies directed at faculty and graduate students—may, despite their detail or specificity, require a faculty imprimatur.)

3. *The librarian and the academic department.* If the relationship between faculty and librarian is sensitive at the campus level, it may be even more critical at the level of an individual department or professional school. Various approaches have been useful in bridging that gap. The collection specialist or branch librarian should, at the least, be invited to attend faculty meetings at which relevant issues are discussed, and that standard may bar participation only in promotion and tenure and perhaps a few other sensitive or unrelated topics. Where it is appropriate, the specialist or branch librarian may even be given faculty status within the department—the more so if (as is often the case) the librarian actually does instruct new graduate students in bibliographic methods or otherwise makes a pedagogical contribution to the school or department. In some fields—law, for example—the library director must be a full-fledged member of the faculty. In that way, the link between library and teaching faculty is ensured. Comparable policies, including less formal links, may be suitable elsewhere.

4. *The library and other academic support programs.* Not many years ago, the library was virtually the only component in a category now somewhat bureaucratically described as "academic support." Today, the academic computing center has become a worthy, if not awesome, competitor. Disciplines that give higher priority to computing or other resources than to traditional library materials may pose for the library and library-dependent faculties a new and increasingly ominous challenge. It is the university administrator's responsibility to mediate fairly and equitably among competing claimants. Both budgetary and personnel support for the computing center and the library must be balanced—even at times when the costs of both are likely to increase faster

than the general inflationary rate. In the process, computer scientists, chemists, and others may feel their needs have been slighted to protect the library; at the same time, the historians, philosophers, and other humanists may look with equal disfavor at the rapidly rising budget for computing. Perhaps the wisest approach is simply to encourage dialogue between faculties in both types of disciplines, making sure that each has adequate information concerning the needs and claims of the other.

5. *The library and the larger community.* Particularly in a small city or town, the university library may be an intellectual resource extending far beyond the campus. Especially where any citizen may borrow books from the university library — at Indiana University, for example — by producing a resident driver's license, the library's impact on the larger community may be substantial. Quite apart from the interlibrary loan service, which a major university collection typically serves, the personal contact with many thousands of citizens (including high school students and students at smaller colleges) may greatly enhance public support for the university generally and for its library collections in particular. Obviously, the problems of enforcement and retrieval are compounded by such a generous lending policy. Nonetheless, the resulting goodwill — not to say enhancement of learning for the larger community — may more than repay the tangible costs and potential losses.

6. *The library and intellectual freedom.* Something surely ought to be said about the university library as a guardian of intellectual freedom. Of course, the university library seldom, if ever, experiences the kinds of censorship pressures to which school and public libraries have recently been subjected with increasing frequency. Nonetheless, requests for lists of borrowers and other, subtler constraints are not unknown. In times of security consciousness and inhibitions upon free inquiry, the university library should offer a haven for and repository of free thought and speech. Anyone who seeks to probe the frontiers of knowledge and learning — however bizarre, unorthodox, or threatening — should find that opportunity most especially in the great university libraries.

The foregoing list of issues obviously omits some to which other administrators might have called attention: the relationship between the university library and schools of library or information science, faculty status and tenure for professional librarians, the sensitive relationship between professional staff and support staff, professional and career development for university librarians, policies for review and approval of library allocation budgets, audiovisual materials in the university library, and many others. Such a list is necessarily selective. The half-dozen issues identified and discussed briefly here are simply those that appear most current and critical to one university administrator. Acknowledgment of its incompleteness should suffice and may serve to challenge others to broaden the scope.

Issues at the National Level

During the past two years, the Association of American Universities and the Council on Library Resources have collaborated on a highly relevant project — a remarkable shared commitment by the presidents of the fifty major American research universities and the organization that has for a quarter century been chiefly responsible for garnering and allocating private support for library projects. Under the general aegis of a joint steering committee, five task forces were constituted in the spring of 1981 to address the topics of preservation, resource sharing, bibliographic systems, technology, and administration and personnel. (Each of these themes will be more fully developed elsewhere in this volume.) The five task forces each included university administrators (typically one president and one or two academic vice-presidents, graduate deans, and so on), one or two faculty members, and one or two library directors or deans. Each group held at least two meetings and most met three times or even four. Each of the task forces received substantial material bearing on its particular focus and framed specific recommendations, proposals, and options for consideration by the steering committee and others. Initially, some thought had been given to convening a national conference for review and evaluation of the proposals emerging from the task forces. Such a summit conference has, however, seemed possibly premature; until the general framework emerges more clearly from the task force studies, it has seemed wiser to proceed more modestly.

At the very least, the work of the steering committee and the five task forces has enhanced the awareness of the nation's major university administrators with respect to problems of which they were previously rather sketchily informed. Preservation provides a cogent example. Most university administrators are vaguely aware of a serious preservation problem that jeopardizes large and irreplaceable portions of their library collections. Yet the gravity of the problem is not well understood by most nonlibrarians. Nor is there a clear perception of the solutions, including their feasibility, desirability, and cost. The focus of the preservation task force has, therefore, served to bring the problem home in concrete terms to many administrators who for years have somehow hoped it would simply vanish or at least could be left to librarians and other specialists to resolve.

One other recent development at the national level deserves particular mention here. During the summer of 1981, a small group (of which this author was a member) reported to the board of the Council on Library Resources on issues facing academic and research libraries in the 1980s. This committee examined closely the current status, prospects, and problems of the research library — especially in the context of changing technologies, rising costs, personnel needs, and other factors of inescapable importance. The report then addressed a broad range of issues: national commitment to library services; libraries' responses to diversity of information media and services; organization or infrastructure of the library community; introduction, diffusion, and financing of new technologies; enhancement of the user–library relationship; and librarianship as a professional career field.

The special committee then offered responses to each of these topics and framed for the board of the council a set of recommendations. Specifically, the committee urged that the council should in the years ahead "enlarge its scope of responsibility" in several specific dimensions:

- Working directly with both the commercial information-knowledge industry (including the publishing industry) and the Library Community to enhance the capabilities of each to serve the library user in appropriate ways,
- Obtaining the assistance of financial analysts in developing options for financing library services. This will include options for allocating service costs and for addressing the questions associated with treating library services as a free public good,
- Assisting the Library Committee to evaluate its present infrastructure in terms of the demands of the 1980s; and, if appropriate, to facilitate changes in this infrastructure that will allow the research and academic libraries to continue to be major contributors to scholarship and education in our society,
- Assisting in the establishment by libraries of cooperative arrangements for the sharing of collection resources. Such cooperative arrangements will take into account considerations such as geography, quality and equality of services, and financing mechanisms,
- Determining the expectations as well as the needs of the individual library user so that these can be reflected in demands to the Library Community as well as to the commercial enterprises, and
- Collaborating with the Library of Congress and other national groups that represent specific aspects of library interests and fostering and encouraging effective international cooperation [Special Committee of the Council on Library Resources, pp. 32–34].

Obviously, these proposals present a major challenge not only for the Council on Library Resources but for the research library community as well. The years ahead demand a thoughtful response to the opportunities, the challenges, the problems, and the pressures that place such a high priority on the library among the university administrator's concerns.

Reference

Special Committee of the Council on Library Resources. "Research and Academic Libraries: An Action Agenda for the 1980s: A Report to the Board of the Council on Library Resources." Unpublished report of the Special Committee of the Council on Library Resources, Washington, D.C., Oct. 1981.

Robert M. O'Neil is president of the University of Wisconsin system.

Everybody knows that libraries need more money, but an
even greater need, librarians say, is for understanding.

What the Academic Librarian
Wants from Administrators
and Faculty

William A. Moffett

At a recent annual meeting of the American Council on Education, I partici-
pated in a panel discussion convened to explore the question of what it is that
librarians expect of faculty and administrators and vice versa. In attempting to
speak on behalf of my professional colleagues, I had sought advice from a wide
range of academic librarians across the country and from virtually every type
of postsecondary institution. It was clear from the scores of thoughtful letters I
received that my correspondents felt that the subject urgently merited consideration. Indeed, it was clear from the tone of some of them that many of my
fellow directors felt they had received considerably less support than they
needed from their institutional colleagues, especially given the central role the
library has been traditionally called upon to play in higher education.

    I had invited librarians to identify the traits, practices, attitudes, and
procedures of the administrative and teaching colleagues they valued most—
the ones that afforded them the most assistance—and to pinpoint those that
had proved the most troublesome. The latter predictably produced a number
of disagreeable misadventures: stories of administrators who tended to see the
library budget as a kind of reserve fund for meeting emergencies; of library

T. Galvin, B. Lynch (Eds.). *New Directions for Higher Education: Priorities for Academic Libraries*, no. 39.
San Francisco: Jossey-Bass, September 1982.

14

facilities designed without the professional advice of the prospective occu-
pants; of the assignment of building space to nonlibrary use without due consideration of the library's own needs; of changes in library services mandated
by faculty and administrators unable or unwilling to provide funds to meet the
financial impact; and of faculty members who chronically gummed up
reserves and browbeat the staff.

To be sure, my correspondents generally took a positive approach.
Most did not cite horror stories or, if they did, were as likely to confess that
such things occurred when the librarian had not adequately done his or her
job—that is, the job of educating one's colleagues about the library, what it is,
how it operates, what kind of support it needs. There was a clear consensus
about what kind of support is needed most, and it is not in the first instance
financial. Although the environment in which we work has been tremendously
affected by runaway inflation, rapid technological change, and new professional initiatives, and although librarians need funds to ensure access to an
ever-expanding body of recorded information, to secure the advantages of
interinstitutional cooperation, and to enable them to make wise use of those
new technologies, my correspondents agreed that, above all, librarians require
the kind of collegial trust and understanding upon which ultimately the quality
of their own service to the institution depends.

Perhaps it goes without saying—although few of my correspondents
failed to mention it—that librarians would like to find in the key individuals in
their institutions those personal characteristics that one always hopes to find
reflected in those with whom we deal: candor, decisiveness, a clear sense of
priorities, balanced judgment, fair mindedness, self-confidence, receptivity,
responsiveness, and warmth. It was reassuring to learn that many librarians
felt those were the very hallmarks of the men and women with whom they had
been associated.

All the same, a signficant number of my fellow directors expressed
anguish and even some despair, and it is my purpose in this chapter to give
voice to their concern. For librarians expect of their teaching and administrative colleagues (and do not invariably find) (1) a genuine understanding of the
library's mission in higher education, (2) a clearer recognition of the professional librarian's craft and an acceptance of the librarian as a peer in the educational enterprise, and (3) a reliable flow of communication and consultation.

Understanding the Library's Mission

Many years ago Lyle (1963) pointed out that the principal deterrent to
good library service is apathy: "administrators who think of the library merely
as a distributing center for books, faculty members who are concerned with
their own affairs, and librarians who have accustomed themselves to limita-

tions" (p. 59). It was disconcerting now to hear from a distinguished academic librarian in New England that "the most pervasive attitude toward the library that I've encountered is benign neglect. Nothing overtly subversive, nothing openly hostile, just a certain amount of indifference, impatience, and a lack of understanding of the complexity of library activity and of the importance of the library as a means for academic excellence." This experience was apparently shared by a California librarian who observed that academic administrators he had known often exhibited a set attitude that "reflects a hope that the library will not cause any trouble, that the library will not need any more funds than it currently receives, that somehow the library will manage to stay in the space it now occupies, and that it should manage to placate those irascible faculty members." And from a Midwestern university a librarian wrote, "It has been my experience that the dean or vice president of academic administration who understands college and/or university libraries is a very rare specimen. I have encountered only one. The library's presence is accepted as a given, but it is not seen as a vital resource for the intellectual endeavors of the institution. Thus, we take our cuts and reductions or make do with marginal allocations without the correlative understanding on the part of the administration as to the meaning of those cuts for academic activity."

Such attitudes stand in sharp contrast to the familiar bromides about the library being the "heart of the campus." Indeed, clichés get in the way of a clear understanding of the library's mission. One cliché particularly rouses the mistrust of librarians, and a former New York colleague shared with me his response to an academic vice-president who had explained his attitude toward the library by saying, "I love books!" The librarian had replied:

> I have nothing against the love of books, *per se*. I, too, love books (or, some of them), but over the years I've developed a healthy skepticism toward applicants for library positions who express this sentiment in support of their applications. The expressed love of books seldom accurately reflects the applicants' potential for effective performance as library workers. One can love books with a passion, yet misunderstand completely what a library is all about. I won't belabor the point, but I also feel misgivings when a senior administrator of the College falls back upon this statement of value. Certainly, it displays a bias in favor of the library's chief physical commodity, but it gives no assurance of understanding that the library is a complex web of relationships of which books are only a part [Personal communication, 1981].

His own proffered alternative slogan was, "We require a predictable flow of information," admittedly not an elegant phrase but one that is a better key to the varied and increasingly sophisticated activities the modern academic library is called upon to perform. These include:

- constructing reliable and comprehensive tools of accessing information, such as card catalogs and indexes to periodicals,
- storing and retrieving information stored in print, microform, and
computerized data bases,
- providing bibliographic instruction,
- supporting both traditional and interdisciplinary research,
- and, yes, preserving the contents of old and deteriorating books,

just to suggest some of the more obvious activities.

In the midst of all the variables and uncertainties that beset colleges
and universities today and the competing claims that vie for the attention of
faculty and administrators, the fact remains that the integrity of the library
will be a leading concern of any institution vitally concerned with the quality
of its educational program. When imaginative development and wise utilization of its library resources are not seen as indispensable to instructional and
research programs throughout the entire spectrum of disciplines, frustration is
inevitably ahead for the librarian. One prominent West Coast director con-
fessed: "The worst situation I can conceive of is to report to a boss who has no
concept of what a unversity library is." Although the same person pointed out
that he had been fortunate to have provosts of "uncanny understanding,"
clearly that good fortune has not been universally shared.

Recognition of the Librarian as a Peer

It has been a long-standing observation that when the mission of the
library is itself not well understood, the role of the librarian is invariably confused and undervalued. A librarian in Florida wrote that in her experience
"faculty and administrative perceptions of that role often put librarians somewhere between secretaries and warehouse supervisors." Another suggested
that administrators typically fail to appreciate the range and complexity of
librarians' responsibilities and tend to dismiss them as rather priviledged
members of the faculty, while at the same time many teachers regard them as
technicians and bureaucrats who have little grasp of what the "real faculty" do.
In that limbo, the librarian is condemned to the isolation of being neither peer
nor collaborator.

Such isolation severely undermines the director who is attempting to
cope with long-range financial planning and short-term budget crises, to make
decisions about rapidly developing computer technologies, to respond to the
challenge of participative management and the demands of state and federal
agencies, and to interact on a continuing basis with comptroller and registrar,
alumni and departmental leaders, union officials and campus police, vendors
and custodians. This director is simultaneously trying to improve and implement fundamental programs in collection development, preservation of

materials, and the education of library users in the skills necessary to survive and prosper in an information-based, postindustrial society.

One director who has served several institutions said that what had been most useful to her had been "the unstated assumption on the part of my president and/or academic vice-president that (1) I know what I am doing, have a level of expertise not available elsewhere in the University and sufficiently developed to be a reliable base for top-level decision making, and where I do not have the necessary expertise, am wise enough to surround myself with staff who do, and (2) that the president (or academic vice-president, etc.) will then solicit my advice, pay attention to it, and act upon it. Obviously, for my part, I must supply the necessary knowledge and credibility upon which such faith is founded."

Quite apart from recognizing the professional expertise of the librarian, a wise president will utilize directors who have a broad overview of the college or university to help with the growing burden of general administrative affairs. And as a respected colleague has pointed out, business, scientific, and industrial research communities have begun to recognize that librarians (or information managers) should be part of their teams, expecially with the proliferation of data bases: "The same should be true of colleges and universities. I've seen so much time wasted simply because no one bothered to search the literature—something librarians would have done right away."

Then there is the reluctance of some faculty members to embrace us as peers, regardless of whatever official status in campus governance may have been accorded to professional librarian. I cherish the wry comment of a Southern librarian who wrote: "By and large faculty members do not know what to make of librarians. There is with most, I think, a tendency to think of us as having a priestly function which other administrators (say, registrars or deans of students) do not [have]. Quite frequently at social functions when the conversation lags a faculty member will blurt out, 'I don't get by the library as often as I should,' and I solemnly grant absolution." Some professional librarians who have been treated as clerks by teaching faculty will accept the priestly function when they can get it—along with the opportunity to mingle at social functions.

Is there a relationship between active scholarly use of the library by faculty members and their respect for the librarian's craft, their understanding of library problems, and their willingness to be helpful in dealing with them? Perhaps so. Teachers who relate the scholarship of their discipline to the graphic record are more likely, one liberal arts college librarian suggests, to base the teaching of their discipline on library resources and services:

> They [faculty members] will have a realistic sense of the problems librarians confront in introducing research techniques and the organization of the bibliographic record to young people who typically have

had little or no training in library resources or techniques in secondary school. They will also understand that library usage does not involve only narrow technical skills but has a substantial intellectual dimension, and that bibliographic organization is a complex matter which requires patience and systematic effort to master. And finally they will understand that any organization must have rules to run effectively, and that most of us are not petty bureaucrats; they will respond to our communications and cooperate in our mutual efforts to build collections and serve the academic community.

On the other hand, it is the inactive scholar, some librarians say, who is most likely to show indifference or condescension or even hostility. The director at one of our most prestigious universities maintains that "the really great scholars, by and large, are the most grateful for library resources and the most respectful of the rights of others," although he admits ruefully that "even in great universities such scholars are few in number." It is invariably the faculty member who has not submitted a book order in the past three years, says a Colorado librarian, "who screams about the books we don't have." It is the faculty member who enters the library infrequently who seems most offended by requirements to show an identification card at the check-out desk, who complains loudest about copyright restrictions or about having to return overdue materials for the use of another patron. Is it lack of familiarity that breeds contempt?

One is frankly appalled by the extent to which there seem to be adversarial relationships between faculty and librarians on some college and university campuses—a condition likely to prove even more troublesome in the future as it becomes more difficult to make decisions about the allocation of resources. Clearly, adversarial relationships thrive where there is not a recognition of the commonality of purpose. One successful Midwestern librarian explained how his academic deal ensures that recognition from the outset: "On the itinerary of every prospective faculty member is a meeting with me or one of the other librarians. That says something to new faculty about the importance of the library, and it also provides the dean and the department with another perspective for hiring. I am also asked to talk with all new faculty during new faculty orientation and that, too, says something about the library."

Communications and Consultation

Opportunities to say something about the library are not everywhere as readily available as one might think. Although on each campus it properly falls to the director to articulate the library's mission and to cultivate recognition of the professional staff as peers and collaborators of the faculty and administration, to do so effectively requires reliable channels of communication. Of great importance, too, are the various informal occasions for contacts in which one's personal skills can come into play. As much as anything, say librarians, one needs a certain attitude on the part of key administrators to create a consultative atmosphere, a willingness to listen. As one university librarian wrote: "The willingness to learn about and explore together the library's needs has been essential to my effectiveness, but it has been indispensable in longer range planning. To know that this condition can be relied upon over a foreseeable future establishes a floor of confidence on which we can build policy and consider new approaches. To be forever doubtful about the reception awaiting new ideas can easily be a nightmare."

Obviously it is important that the librarian not only be heard but also be told what is going on, what is possible, and what is not. Most major decisions in colleges and universities ultimately have an effect upon the library, and no one has greater reason than the librarian to plead, "No secrets, no surprises!" Early warnings of likely changes in curriculum, of budget reductions, and of expanding or contracting programs is essential for the long-range planning a librarian has to do. Indeed, warning may be too weak a word; consultation prior to decisions is clearly advisable if the institution is to make use of the librarian's unique perspectives. Yet in practice it seems to have been rarely the norm, and as we enter a period of rapidly developing crises, it could become even less likely.

On many campuses the flow of communications has been hampered for the librarian by the very way in which the central administration is organized. To whom should the librarian report? The proliferation of central management staff in the 1960s has nearly severed the direct access that chief librarians once had to the president. In many cases, the new layer of offices interposed between the librarian and the president has seriously reduced the library's opportunity to present its case; the librarian on such campuses is less likely to participate in making decisions about institutional policy.

However, I found few librarians who in 1981 felt that direct and frequent access to the president was necessary. More than one recognized that the top executive was "so busy that opportunities to discuss library programs in a meaningful and extended manner were infrequent." What I did find was almost unanimous agreement that the librarian should be able to bring problems immediately and directly to the chief academic officer, whoever that might be, and not have to filter them through several layers of bureaucracy. If the administrator to whom the librarian reports does not have the authority to make decisions, set priorities, and allocate resources, the librarian often has trouble getting promptly to the person who makes decisions. Many correspondents described the frustration they had experienced in dealing with vice-presidents or deans who seemed trapped in cumbersome bureaucracies. One wrote that despite the monthly meetings that gave the librarian an opportunity to review with his superior problems and proposals, final approval of major proposals inevitably "had to be sought by him or by me from other administrators, groups of administrators, or from faculty committees. There were no immediate answers to straightforward questions. In some cases important opportunities were missed; in others additional problems were created by my inability to obtain satisfactory answers quickly. Staff morale was adversely affected by what seemed to be the administration's refusals to give legitimate library concerns a high priority."

Although my correspondents seemed to allow for differences in personality and variations of style that shape the reporting structure differently from campus to campus, there was general consensus that there should be structured, regularly scheduled meetings with the chief academic officer rather than conferences based on specific situations. The latter approach invariably confines discussion to single issues—often problems requiring immediate attention—rather than broad discussions of the enterprise. Moreover, even when reporting directly to the academic vice-president, some effort should be made to prevent the librarian from being isolated from other members of the administration, especially the various divisional vice-presidents. Regular participation in the president's executive committee or the council of academic deans not only gives the librarian an opportunity to brief fellow administrators on library issues, to learn what is going on, and to contribute to general decisions on policy, but it also affords chances to cultivate personal friendships with other members of the administration, and these can be of crucial importance later.

A number of institutions (led initially, I believe, by Columbia University and the University of Texas) have tried to ensure the librarians' access to and partnership in the university power structure by establishing the director as a vice-president. Some institutions that subsequently adopted this model have experienced difficulties from the tendency to crowd other academic support services under the same umbrella. Although there is some affinity between the academic library, the computing center, and television production facilities, certainly enough to group them under, say, a vice-president for information services, the differences may be more important than the similarities. Certainly there have been instances in which this development has simply further diluted the library's support and moved the bottleneck in administrative communications to another level.

The task of establishing good communications with other administrators, however, may be much less problematic than establishing them with the faculty—especially in a large institution. There the range of personal contacts tends to be limited and the mechanisms for carrying on a continuing dialogue are almost nonexistent. In 1981, representatives from the Association of

Research Libraries and the American Association for the Advancement of the Humanities examined that very problem of scholar-librarian communications in a meeting funded by the Council on Library Resources. Although the concern of the participants was primarily with research libraries, the impediments they cited stand in the way of good communications between faculty and librarians in virtually every type and size of academic institution. Indeed, some are national in nature:

> Lack of information for faculty is a key element. Library journals abound, but there are no consistently convenient descriptions of library issues for the information of scholars. The widespread use of jargon and professional terminology in writings about libraries also hampers the exchange of ideas. New faculty members are often insufficiently prepared in bibliography and library use and do not have a clear understanding of how libraries operate of the problems they face. In many institutions the faculty-library committee — frequently the "official" channel for faculty-library communication — does not attract the aggressive and interested participation required for effectiveness. And finally, there is a tendency among scholars to focus on the library only in crises. Scholars need to be informed not only about problems, but also about new library services and technologies that will affect their research and teaching in the future (Mandel, 1981, p. 00).

The participants argued that the first step must be to "get faculty members to recognize their stake in the library" and the next was to keep them aware of pertinent issues and problems. On a national level, they proposed securing greater visibility for research libraries by reports in society newsletters and journals and by discussions and demonstrations of on-line services at the annual meetings of learned societies. For all that, the group concluded that "individual effort on the parts of both librarians and scholars is still the most effective and most important way to strengthen the link between the faculty and the library." To that end, librarians should not neglect the time-tested opportunities for inviting such efforts from faculty colleagues: campus publications, systems of departmental liaisons, and interaction with the faculty library committee, as well as cultivating the support of individual faculty members.

But will they be encouraged by the faculty's response? My own correspondents listed examples of departmental heads who failed to appoint faculty liaisons to the library and others who ignored the reports of appointed liaisons; of departments that were unwilling to have the director appear at departmental meetings or to work with library staff members assigned as departmental liaisons; of departments that failed to help set goals for collection development

in the literature of their discipline; of faculty members of the library committee who either did not take their charge seriously or who used their position to
interfere in day-to-day operations; and of faculty who made commitments
affecting the library without consulting the director.

All of my colleagues did not report such gloomy anecdotes. One told of
the reaction to her announcement that there would have to be serious cuts in
journal subscriptions:

> A senior faculty member came into my office, banged his fist and said
> that he did not like chemistry journals cut; I had expected that, but I
> did not expect his next two comments, which were, 'But I know you
> have to do it. So what can we do to make the best of it?' This initial dis-
> cussion led to the setting up of the library chemistry task force that
> developed some creative ways of dealing with cuts as well as planning
> for library instruction to make sure that students could take advantage
> of information both in our library and in the area.

And another reported:

> The year before last the chairman of our library advisory committee
> was so impressed with the figures we produced to illustrate the deterio-
> rating economy of this library he decided to write a report on our
> behalf. His initial intention was to direct the report to the president of
> the university and the vice-presidents. He not only did this, but man-
> aged to rework the piece for publication in the library press. It appeared
> in the May 1981 issue of the *Journal of Academic Librarianship*. Surely this
> is unusual dedication to the library cause by a faculty member who also
> happens to be an active scholar and a busy department head.

Unfortunately, the librarian added, this faculty member's willingness to communicate what he had learned about the library and to see the library in an
institution-wide rather than a departmental context was exceptional.

Conclusion

There is another side to this, we know. Communications may falter,
cooperation may remain less than adequate, and the mission of the library
may tend to be dimly perceived on some campuses because of failings on
the part of the librarian. The aim of this chapter, however, has not been to
examine the shortcomings of my own counterparts, any more than it has been
to congratulate those of us who enjoy high levels of understanding and support. Over the years there has been no shortage of articles, workshops, and
speeches — both analytical and hortatory — addressing the urgent challenges of

leadership and management facing chief librarians. They are challenges few of us have an opportunity to forget for long; we are routinely and acutely reminded of them by the unfolding of our budget printouts.

The assistance we need from our institutional colleagues, however, has not always been well understood. It is an issue almost never addressed in professional literature. This report, then, is made on behalf of those librarians who can in this way call for help, a call made even more timely by the reassessment of institutional objectives that the pressures of the 1980s are mandating so inexorably. The need for that help was especially well expressed by W. Robert Parks, president of Iowa State University, at the start of a fund drive for his own library in 1978. Speaking of the interdependent nature of the university, he said:

> Scholarship is generally a lonely occupation. But even the work and the achievements of the most solitary scholar are dependent upon the caliber of that network of functioning relationships which is the university. No discipline, no department, no college of the university can stand alone. It cannot achieve the high peaks of nationally recognized excellence and distinction unless it is a part of a disciplinarily interdependent university, known to be strong in the basic areas of knowledge. Moreover, no discipline, no department, no college on this campus can stand apart from the future of the University Library, independently aloof from the problems it is facing. For the quality and worth of every discipline is tied into the quality and worth of the Library's holdings (Parks, 1978, p. 1).

The advancement of the common good of the academic community, Parks concluded, is tied to the ability of the library, even in hard times, to make continuing progress. He noted that danger that "what is everybody's business, becomes nobody's business," and the possibility that the central and long-term good of a college or university can "quite easily become submerged in the intricacies of specialized drives and purposes." The library's needs, he stressed, "must become the shared concern of every scholar and every department on this campus. We must each of us make it our own individual business." To this statement each library director in the country will say, Amen.

References

Lyle, G. R. *The President, the Professor, and the College Library.* New York: Wilson, 1963.
Mandel, C. A. "Report to Directors of ARL Libraries on the AAAH/ARL Meeting on Library/Scholar Communications." Unpublished memorandum, Aug. 1981.
Parks, W. R. "Remarks at a Staff Convocation, Iowa State University." Unpublished presentation at Iowa State University, Ames, Sept. 1978.

24

William A. Moffett is Azariah S. Root director of libraries at Oberlin College.

The expectations of users of library services in the future,
though dimly seen, will focus on both tradition and innovation,
driven by the values of current successes and the advent of the
information age.

New Expectations from
Users of Academic Libraries

Russell Shank

A cardinal rule in marketing is that one should never ask the customer simply what he or she wants. Unless the surveyor offers details of alternative products and services, the answer is likely to be vague, uncertain, and without vision. Or perhaps the answer will take the form of suggestions that are impossible to achieve. So it is with library and information service. The literature is devoid of analytical thoughts from scholars about what they want from libraries, except that there is often some notion that the wonderful world of computers ought to allow us to put the contents of the Library of Congress on the head of a pin and to call up any text in response to any query, from anywhere in the world, to any level of specificity, instantaneously. These may be useful trend indicators of the power of the new information technology in general, but they offer little that can be helpful to librarians in the design and operation of today's libraries.

Even when proposals are seemingly specific, as with Bush (1945) and his "memex" desk, they are often meant only to point out generalities that set vague potential in the context of possible trends. Most library users have in mind the need for an institution that buys books and journals, catalogs them, and makes them available in a timely fashion for some reasonable period. We do have many fine essays, such as those of Shaw (1940) and Butler (1940), on

T. Galvin, B. Lynch (Eds.). *New Directions for Higher Education: Priorities for Academic Libraries,* no. 39.
San Francisco: Jossey-Bass, September 1982.

the manner in which practitioners of certain disciplines use literature or information in the literature. To the extent that librarians have been able to use these analyses to guide collection development and reference services, it has been mostly through a process of inference and deduction based on ideas latent in the essays.

Then there are the fine books from scholars and administrators about academic and research libraries in general, mostly rather old now, which set a grand philosophical tone to what we are and can do. Branscomb (1940) argued brilliantly for the advent of more mechanisms that would bring students and books together. The thesis of his book was that the task of the college library was to assist the attainment of instructional goals of the faculty. Brough (1953) called for a revalidation of the purposes and the functions of the university library and the mounting of a vigorous new attack on its persistent problems. We have been working long on these problems, but until the advent of the computer, we have principally applied new mechanics to mundane goals. (The Farmington plan, for example, created an orderly matrix to a national plan for libraries to use in cooperative collection development, but merely strengthened the hands of the libraries that were already collecting in various disciplines and languages and left the cataloging effort to be done in the only fashion that was then in vogue — the card catalog.)

Ray (1978) argues for the book and its availability in academic libraries as a key support to academic enterprises. This is a durable goal, for, as avid as the new technologists are, the format of the book is a superb technical design for a storage and conveyance device for information to be used in the variety of settings in which individuals may find themselves. Finally, we have the many books, such as that of Fussler (1973), that probe the new world of information technology for its utility to libraries. His is an absolutely essential kind of analysis, even though the emphasis and utility of technology shifts faster and more unpredictably than even the keenest technologist can predict. It is apparent that society is entering an information age, which must have an impact on the very nature of libraries, as they can be described generically.

To determine what users might want from libraries, either in the short run or the long run, we will have to deduce this want from the known habits of scholars and the things we know that libraries can and should do in the new information world. Librarians may thus be telling the user what he or she ought to expect from libraries; this is partly wish fulfillment. Librarians are key agents in the information world, and they won't be left out of the future if they embrace it strongly enough. These professionals know that there is more in the information world that can serve the scholar than anyone other than the librarians knows.

That which follows, therefore, is a mixture of comments about what the seeker after information is likely to expect from an institution in the new age, given the directions in which that age is pushing cultural development, and what those in the profession of librarianship think will or ought to happen to libraries as the information age advances. Libraries could stick to their traditional endeavors, which relate primarily to the book and the journal, and indeed these will continue as long as there are books. We all must expect, however, that there will have to be institutional answers for some of the users' needs for information based on the processing capabilities of the new technology and that the library is the logical and the ready-made institution for this purpose.

Environmental Influences

The basis for speculation about the future of academic library service, which is the subject of this chapter, lies in a judgment about the environment within which higher education will operate for the foreseeable future. This environment is being subjected to strong influences, many of which contain completely unanticipated elements. The book *Future Shock* (Toffler, 1970) is only twelve years old, yet it did not foresee the microcomputer invasion of the home.

It would be the height of arrogance, therefore, to state with assurance too many details about the social setting for higher education even a few years hence. But certain trends suggest some inevitable general conclusions. These are presented here to provide a sounder understanding of the succeeding statements about library service.

American society will be subjected to social and fiscal conservatism long enough to make some basic differences between the structure and content of today's higher educational experiences and those of the future. In addition, certain demographic characteristics of society will have an impact on higher education. Assuredly, the number of young people of college age will be less for a generation than it has been. It is quite probable that more older people will be interested in some aspects of higher education. Although continuing education at the college level has long been a viable function, the number of people opting for this activity will increase, either merely because there are more of them or because colleges and universities will seek them out to sustain their facilities (Watkins, 1982). More students may enroll for part-time studies, particularly if they are older and involved in jobs and family activities.

It also appears that there will be a continuation of the movement of students to the professional and vocational subjects (Carnegie Foundation for the Advancement of Teaching, 1977). This will have an obvious impact on academic libraries, particularly the large ones with many other subject interests. More book funds will have to be allocated for the professional fields. If fiscal constraints do not allow for an increase in the total book budget, this emphasis can only take place by a reprogramming of the funds away from the humanities. In addition, there will be a continued intake of students who may have trouble with basic learning skills such as reading, writing, and mathematics. This, too, might lead to an expectation that academic libraries will devote some of their resources to propaedeutic materials or expand their undergraduate resources to contain more alternative media for students with varying learning abilities.

Perhaps the strongest and most pervasive influence on higher education is the ever-spreading use of electronic utilities and devices. This influence can be characterized in a number of ways, but, in the main, the analyses of Bell (1973) and Toffler (1980), which argue that we are well into the decline of the industrial age and the rise of the electronic age, provide all the intellectual room needed for speculation about the society of the future. The electronic age brings the handling of data and information to center stage, hence it directly and soundly affects such information-bound activities as education.

Finally (for this analysis), we can expect an increasing sophistication in the laws and regulations that affect information activities. These are likely to bear directly on the extent, the timing, and the manner in which educational functions such as those performed by libraries will adopt the new technologies to respond to users' expectations.

General Expectations

With these influences in mind, we might well predict the following expectations about the shape of the library in the near future. People will be oriented more toward information and access to it than to the media in which the information is contained. As the television screen and the cathode-ray computer monitor become more ubiquitous, information by the screenful may become a predominant expectation. Thus, whether the user is getting the contents of a computer file rather than a page of text will lose relevance. In other words, the book or any other medium will be less relevant to many users than the information it contains. Librarians will be expected to work as easily with the nonprint media as they do with books and journals. Library users may be less tolerant of librarians' uneasiness in this environment or may simply reject those of us who cannot work naturally and easily with the new media.

Obviously, if libraries work with more media and means of access to information, they will have to be well supplied with the equipment required to use the new formats, and library staffs will be expected to be at ease with the use of this equipment. The burden will not be on the librarian alone. Libraries will become more complicated environments for the user. Although people may be more at ease as time passes with computer terminals, microform readers, recording monitors, playback machines, and more, the specifics of their installation and linkages in libraries and their ties to various formats of materials will increase the sophistication of the library. The array of equipment and the strategies for finding information will not be self-apparent. The user should expect to spend time learning how to work in the new information environment. The library, therefore, should be expected to have a strong program of instruction on library use. This will require an enhancement of the librarian's teaching abilities and will make that portion of the librarian's job more prominent. We should all pay close attention, therefore, to the literature on bibliographic instruction, such as that listed by Lockwood (1979).

Libraries will have to increase their interaction with each other on the users' behalf. Our concern with networks, so aptly spelled out by Markuson and Woolls (1980), will continue and grow. Fiscal conservatism will make cooperation among libraries seem more appealing, and electronic facilities can serve this interaction well. There is, however, a caveat that librarians and academic instructors must face: Both the development of interactive mechanisms and their operation are not cheap. We have much work yet to do in the area of cost comparisons of various means of accessing books and information. This will be most difficult, and not only because it is a complex task. A new library system supported by electronic technology will likely result in an increase in the kind, amount, and quality of the functions and services the library can perform, thus increasing its appeal to users and its operating cost.

The true measure of the need for library service in the academic institution, then, becomes one of the value of a total information environment to the qualities the campuses are trying to achieve. This requires a commitment by librarians and administrators just at a time when the fiscal situation is bleak enough to block out thoughts of new programs and increased development costs.

Even if these potentials cannot yet be contemplated, fiscal conservatism will force change. The budgets of academic libraries will be pared in the immediate future along with those of the institutions in which they serve. Library users have a right to expect that their libraries are operating as economically and as efficiently as possible before changes due to fiscal constraints are introduced. Tight budgets emphasize the need for an analysis of the functions of an academic library; knowledge of the design and control of the processes in the library will also be vital. With so many competing sources of information being introduced to the public, the primacy of the library may be threatened unless it can accommodate to change. The user should expect that the library will be a different place than tradition has built.

More specifically, research libraries will grow more slowly than they have for the past thirty years. A core of material to support current teaching and research will always be available, but some part of the fringe material — the large collection of esoteric archives and older books and tracts, the sets of exceedingly highly specialized journals, the many obscure foreign pamphlets, and the like — will not be as widely held among as many libraries as at present. The user should expect that more planning will be required to conduct scholarly studies, to allow for travel to distant collections, or to pay for their filming for transport to the local library. One of the chief professional functions of the librarian of the future will undoubtedly have to be assisting the user in the development of an information-seeking strategy. Ownership of much research material by a library will be deemphasized in favor of delivery of the material to the user from whatever source it can be obtained. Timeliness of access for the user is the key element, and its determination will strengthen the need for closer interaction between the user and the library than ever before.

A corollary to this is that libraries may have to serve more secondary users as a matter of course. The success of library cooperation in acquisitions will be directly proportional to the willingness and the ability, legally and financially, for the library to open its stacks to shared use by scholars and students from other institutions and the willingness and ability of the user to travel to the resources (or wait for their delivery if this can be accomplished). In other words, cooperative acquisition in libraries is not the same as sharing of resources. These are two separate functions that must be planned together. This style of operation is not foreign either to libraries or to scholars, but it will have to become more prevalent (Shank, 1976).

The demographic changes previously mentioned portend some expectations that are not basically profound, but will demand an awareness by librarians. Part-time students require longer loan periods for library materials than do their peers among the full-time student body. Older students and others who may work or have stronger commitments elsewhere than on campus may require a different schedule of library hours that may be difficult to manage. Yet if the educational experience for them is to be of the caliber offered to their full-time colleagues, they will expect libraries to accommodate them. These people may well expect more remote access to information about library collections in order better to plan their campus visits and thus may be primary proponents of electronic communication capabilities in libraries.

Advent of the Electronic Age

Among all of the societal influences for change in libraries and in the manner in which scholarship and teaching are performed, the advent of the electronic age is the strongest. It is bound to cause the most profound changes and the most disruption in the ways in which scholars work, in teaching, and in studying. It will, however, offer such compelling capabilities to make these changes and to work in the new mode that it will be an attractive and irresistible force. Libraries cannot avoid using the computer and telecommunications utilities, and teachers can overlook them only at the jeopardy of being completely isolated from their students, who have grown up familiar with the information world. The potential for changed expectations among the users for access to the new information technology will by high.

The Changing Profession. As librarians have access to more electronic information delivery and handling mechanisms, they will be in a position to respond more quickly and fully to patrons' needs. The traditional image of the library and the librarian should fade and be replaced by an information utility and professional operator from which the user ought to and will expect more service; the focus of the library will increasingly be on information. The format and location of the source of the information ought to be less important to the user than the information itself.

If the electronic journal becomes prevalent, the user may expect the library to be an agent of the "publisher," producing text on demand rather than holding it ready for distribution in the stacks. If this mode of communication of scholarly information becomes the acceptable way for research information to be placed on the market, libraries will not be able to avoid this expectation from their users.

Productivity. Electronic information processing and communication hardware and software will greatly increase the productivity of the library worker. Furthermore, not only will the worker be able to perform the basic work more efficiently but also the library will be able to offer more services than ever before. The user should expect to benefit. Library materials should be obtained faster and be available sooner once acquired than in the traditional library. The user should be able to receive tailored bibliographies and lists of newly acquired materials quickly, easily, and as often as library funding can provide.

Fiscal Interests. This improvement of productivity is nicely matched to the pressures of the fiscally conservative economy. Actually, fewer people should be needed to perform the technical tasks in libraries, and more should be available for user services. Unfortunately, present experience is that the savings from automated procedures is hardly sufficient to match the withdrawal of funds from the academic enterprise because of fiscal restrictions. Also, there is thus insufficient staff to mine the system and refine the information in it for the user in spite of the sometimes spectacular potential of the electronic mechanisms. Without an agreement within an institution of the total function of the library and its funding adequate to the goal, libraries may not be able to deliver all that is expected of them.

The power of electronic-based information facilities is and will continue to be most attractive. Most libraries, however, will be unable to fund the operation of enough capability to satisfy all of their users' demands. Users, therefore, most expect to share some of the burden of covering the costs of the installation and the use of the new information technology. They ought not to expect, however, to pay for the right to obtain basic library services. These services must still be supported by institutional budgets. Somewhere the line must be drawn between the basic services, even if they are the products of automation, and those that extend the library's power beyond this base. The user may be expected to pay the cost of special service. Schools may have to subsidize those who are less financially able, but who still need the full range of services for academic success. (Ackoff and others; 1976), even propose that funds be allocated to users, not to libraries. Users would then shop for information. Libraries would survive only if they could attract paying customers.)

Electronic Bibliography. The traditional card catalog is already disappearing in many libraries. It is rapidly being replaced by microform lists of the libraries' holdings or *on-line,* computer-based catalogs. An on-line catalog is the modern version of a traditional library card catalog. The traditional library card catalog consists of wooden trays containing three-by-five-inch cards representing authors, titles and subjects of books in the library's collection. When the traditional card catalog is replaced by an on-line catalog, names of authors, book titles, and book subjects are stored in a computer and displayed to the library user at a computer terminal. Many academic libraries are currently in the process of substituting computer-output-microform catalogs or on-line catalogs for traditional card catalogs. The user, therefore, must expect to develop entirely new habits in searching for information in the library. In this activity, the library may well have preceded the demand from scholars and students. If libraries were not automating, the growing number of users who have begun to work with home computers and who are fans of video arcades most assuredly would have driven libraries to adopt the same technology. As it is, the two trends may happily be merging.

As on-line catalogs develop, users will undoubtedly demand remote access, from their offices or homes, to the electronic files that libraries will offer in lieu of today's card catalogs. Libraries must expect that the public will press for a greater degree of integration of the many files and systems that we may develop or use.

Legal and Regulatory Influences

In spite of the federal administration's drive to reduce the influence of government through a reduction of regulation, the shift of power to the states in the new federalism will likely sustain, if not increase, the amount of law and regulation that institutions will have to contend with. Accountability is too much a part of the current web of society. It may be harder to do without the supervision at the local level than at the federal level.

A likely increase in unionism in libraries will complicate management.

changes in job content and the way in which work is performed will become more subject to negotiation, which may slow down the advent of electronics in libraries. (This is not meant to be an argument against unions, but merely a statement of what will happen in libraries. The move to the electronic world is inevitable.)

The introduction of new electronic computer and telecommunications technology is a major business venture and will require considerable capital. Furthermore, this segment of industry is particularly heavily impacted by the federal, state, and local government. The various potential operators of the business are engaged in major struggles for access and control of various sectors of the enterprise. (The spread of cable television was markedly slowed by federal and local regulations during the 1970s. At present both the federal government and the American Telephone & Telegraph company are engaged in negotiating the future of that industrial giant. The future of competition in information technology is at stake.) The major point to be made here is that in spite of the wonders of the new technology, it is a long way from the idea to the market, and there is no predicting when the library world will be able to offer the full potential of information technology to the users.

Among other things, we have done an inadequate job of creating the "electronic copyright." Intellectual property in electronic systems will have to be protected. Somehow the costs of developing and installing systems of access to machine-readable information will have to be covered. Libraries may expect to have to pay for access to such information, which they may not hold or may hold only in electronic formats, just as they now pay for the cost of book acquisition. For some exceptional uses of this literary property, the user will have to pay. The whole future of the transfer of payments from the user to the generator of information will have to change.

Libraries stand today in exactly the same relationship between the publisher and the reader as they did when they were founded. But there are now more publishers of more kinds of media with different means of getting information to the user than ever before. The role of the library has thus been diluted. The ultimate place and function of the library in the midst of the new world of information institutions is only dimly seen. The boundaries between sectors of the information agencies will shift and become less clear (Compaine, 1981).

In spite of the great enthusiasm for information technology and its potential utility in education and information services, Norwood (1980) reminds us that the millenium has not arrived. The power of this technology and the recommendations for its use that appeared in the report by the Carnegie Commission on Higher Education (1972) have been far from achieved or even recognized. Nevertheless, there has already been change in the use of information technology by libraries. Lynch (1982) reminds us that, just as libraries have accommodated and changed in the past, they will continue to do so even if it is only to make incremental, short-range moves toward large, long-range changes.

References

Ackoff, R., and others. *Designing a National Scientific and Technological Communication System: The SCATT Report.* Philadelphia: University of Pennsylvania Press, 1976.

Bell, D. *Coming of Post-Industrial Society: A Venture in Social Forecasting.* New York: Basic Books, 1973.

Branscomb, H. *Teaching with Books: A Study of College Libraries.* Chicago: American Library Association, 1940.

Brough, K. *Scholar's Workshop: Evolving Concepts of Library Service.* Urbana: University of Illinois Press, 1953.

Bush, V. "As We May Think." *Atlantic Monthly,* 1945, *176,* 101–108.

Butler, P. "The Research Worker's Approach to Books—the Humanist." In W. Randall (Ed.), *The Acquisition and Cataloging of Books.* Chicago: University of Chicago Press, 1940.

Carnegie Commission on Higher Education. *The Fourth Revolution: Instructional Technology in Higher Education.* New York: McGraw-Hill, 1972.

Carnegie Foundation for the Advancement of Teaching. *Missions of the College Curriculum: A Contemporary Review with Suggestions.* San Francisco: Jossey-Bass, 1977.

Compaine, B. M. "Shifting Boundaries in the Information Marketplace." In C. Rochell (Ed.), *An Information Agenda for the 1980s.* Chicago: American Library Association, 1981.

Fussler, H. H. *Research Libraries and Technology: A Report to the Sloan Foundation.* Chicago: University of Chicago Press, 1973.

Lockwood, D. *Library Instruction: A Bibliography.* Westport, Conn.: Greenwood, 1979.

Lynch, B. "Options for the 80s: Directions in Academic and Research Library Development." *College and Research Libraries,* 1982, *43* (2), 124–129.

Markuson, B., and Woolls, B. *Networks for Networkers: Critical Issues in Cooperative Library Development.* New York: Neal-Schuman, 1980.

Norwood, F. W. "Telecommunications and Education in the 1980s." *Journal of Library Automation,* 1980, *13* (4), 281–282.

Ray, G. "A Retrospective View." In E. C. Latham (Ed.), *American Libraries as Centers of Scholarship.* Hanover, N.H.: Dartmouth College, 1978.

Shank, R. "The Locus for Cooperation in Collections Sharing." In *The Responsibility of the University Library Collection in Meeting the Needs of its Campus and Local Community.* La Jolla: Friends of the University of California, San Diego Library, 1976.

Shaw, R. R. "The Research Worker's Approach to Books—the Scientist." In W. Randall (Ed.), *The Acquisition and Cataloging of Books.* Chicago: University of Chicago Press, 1940.

Toffler, A. *Future Shock.* New York: Random House, 1970.

Toffler, A. *The Third Wave.* New York: Morrow, 1980.

Watkins, B. T. "21 Million Adults Found Taking Part in Continuing Education Programs." *Chronicle of Higher Education,* May 5, 1982, p. 10.

Russell Shank is the university librarian and professor
in the Graduate School of Library and Information Science
at the University of California, Los Angeles.

In the present fiscal climate of higher education, librarians are compelled to work with the budgets they have and to modify the elements of the budgets in order to cope with their changing environment.

Financing the Academic Library

Richard J. Talbot

If libraries are to continue to be a vital part of the academic enterprise, library finance and especially library budgeting must be radically changed. It is not merely a matter of changing amounts on budgetary lines in response to an increase or decrease in demand or supply; the problem is much more fundamental. Librarians must begin to see the budget for what it really is—the fiscal reflection of institutional intent—and act accordingly. The lament for past glories and the wringing of hands about present difficulties, which characterize so much of the debate on present discontent in libraries, must be put aside. Instead, the academic community must define library needs and purposes in useful and pragmatic terms that can be expressed in library budgets at local, regional, and national levels. It is no longer sufficient to regard the budget merely as a source of funds; it is a tool for implementation and decision.

Library Finance

It is only a modest exaggeration to claim that all academic library finance is based on the 5 percent rule: that is, the library should receive 5 percent of the general and educational budget of the parent institution. On the average, since 1968, the percentage of the general and educational budget devoted to libraries has hovered around 3.8 percent. (Beazley, 1981; Osburn, 1979). Of course, there is a fluctuation in the percentage received among any

T. Galvin, B. Lynch (Eds.). *New Directions for Higher Education: Priorities for Academic Libraries*, no. 39.
San Francisco: Jossey-Bass, September 1982.

comparison group of academic libraries. Obviously, some received a greater percentage of the general and educational budget and some libraries received less, but the range seems consistently to lie between 2 and 7 percent (Cohen and Leeson, 1979, for example); large institutions devote a somewhat smaller fraction of their budgets to libraries than some of the smaller, wealthier institutions do.

Why should there be such an astonishing similarity and persistent stability in the fraction of the parent institution's budget that is devoted to libraries? It certainly cannot be based on a direct relationship with some commonly defined academic purpose. If it were, the percentages even among institutions with similar academic purposes would differ sharply, simply because their incomes differ sharply. In other words, if the academic purposes are similar, academic needs including library needs will be similar, and these should require similar levels of funding that, given differences in institutional budgets, ought to require widely different percentages of the general and educational budget, not the similar patterns commonly observed.

The answer is that library finance is a manifestation of imitative behavior. It is not determined by academic need any more than higher education finance in general is determined by institutional need (Bowen, 1980). Colleges and universities are called upon to respond to so many different kinds and levels of need that "no precise need. . . can be objectively defined and defended" (Bowen, 1980, p. 16). To be sure, one can objectively define and defend the need for a particular book at a particular time, but, beyond this level of particularity, Bowen's generalization holds for libraries.

In fact, higher educational unit costs obey Bowen's revenue theory of cost, which states that "an institution's educational cost per student unit is determined by revenues available for educational purposes" (1980, p. 17). These costs are not determined by need, but by funds available; they are driven by the "laws" of higher educational cost. Each institution pursues excellence in an unlimited way by raising and spending all it can, so the result is toward ever-increasing expenditure (Bowen, 1980). It should not be surprising that libraries, which are creatures of their institutions, obey the same laws, since what really explains the stability of the fraction of the budget devoted to libraries is the revenue theory of cost. Moreover, library finance is almost entirely dependent on institutional revenue (Cohen and Leeson, 1979) and, since libraries have a settled place in the firmament of their institutions, they receive their "just" due and no more. Up to now, at least, it has not mattered whether or how library costs change or what new demands they are called upon to meet. On the whole, they still receive only their "fair share" of the institutional pie. The efforts of librarians to define library needs in ways that would enable them to obtain a greater fraction of the budget thus may seem irrelevant.

This does not mean that imitative behavior should be condemned or that the effort to define library needs should be abandoned. Imitation, as a result of comparing one institution with another, may be a practical necessity in dealing with higher budgetary officials who "don't have time for the details" or legislators who may more readily understand such comparisons. It can also be a marketplace response in providing the facilities equivalent to competing institutions in order to attract and retain faculty and students. It may even indicate a kind of latent standard of performance that is imminent in the behavioral patterns of librarians. What imitative behavior in library financing does not do is to provide a rationale for articulating library needs and matching them to the resources needed to meet them.

A more promising approach to defining library needs and, therefore, library budgets in quantitative terms is the development of a mathematical model using actual data rather than the guesses of practitioners. Baumol and Marcus (1973) published a study that applied regression analysis to library data. Their study demonstrated how regression analysis could be used to generate a formula that could, in turn, be used to generate a budget. Since this method is grounded in actual data, it reflects existing conditions, and it can be applied to various groups so that like libraries can be compared to like libraries. Stubbs (1981) carried this line of research farther by using factor analysis on library data. He shows that it is possible to develop empirical criteria that can distinguish between the larger university libraries in the Association of Research Libraries and the smaller ones outside of it. These criteria can be expressed in quantitative terms, which can be used to generate a library budget. They tell us a great deal about such libraries, and they can be useful in making comparisons among them.

Unfortunately, such research, no matter how valuable, begs, the fundamental question. It does not explain, as Stubbs himself notes, why the characteristics of collections, expenditures, and staffing that he analyzed are appropriate as responses to library needs. To do that would require the ability to more closely match library resources to user needs and to pursue the development of measures of library activities, users, and performance that might make such matching possible. Such techniques do not now exist in forms that would enable the library planner to use them effectively. Indeed, it is questionable whether such measures, no matter how desirable, will ever be completely satisfactory or whether they can sufficiently describe the phenomena to be measured to be entirely useful.

Libraries, because they are creatures of their institutions, reflect institutional purposes in frequently obscure ways. They do not merely serve the instructional and research needs of the academic population, although this is usually their basic stated purpose. They also function, for example, as showplaces for the institution or as repositories of special bequests, which may attract the interest and support of donors not only for the library but also for the institution itself. Consequently, efforts to analyze libraries entirely in quantitative terms are bound to fail. Qualitative judgments are ever present, both in the actual delivery of typical library services and in the fulfilling of other institutional purposes that extend a narrow conception of the library.

There is no simple formula, no set of standard techniques that will enable the librarian, unaided, clearly to set forth the financing that is needed in a particular library. No comparisons, however compelling, are likely significantly to change the existing expenditure patterns for libraries in an institution because to do so would require changes in the total expenditure pattern and upset an existing balance. Therefore, librarians will be compelled to work with what they have and to modify the elements of the library budget itself in order to cope with their changing environment.

Library Budgeting

Just as it is only a modest exaggeration to claim that library finance is dominated by the 5 percent rule, it is also only a modest exaggeration to claim that library budgeting—the allocation of funds received by the library—is dominated by the 60–30–10 rule: 60 percent of the library budget is for staff, 30 percent for acquisitions, and 10 percent for other costs. This pattern has persisted for so long that it approximates an historical norm (Beazley, 1981; Cohen and Leeson, 1979). But unlike the stability of the pattern for the percentage of the general and educational budget that libraries receive, there have been fluctuations in the 60–30–10 pattern. Between 1960 and 1979, total dollar expenditures increased and a greater percentage of the library budget was spend on materials than on staff. Salary expenditures as a percentage of the total library budget fell from 61.3 percent in 1960 to 53.8 percent in 1968, while the percentage for materials rose from 29.7 percent in 1960 to 36.4 percent in 1969. After 1969, however, the pattern reversed. The percentage of expenditure for staffing rose from 57 percent in 1970 to 61 percent in 1975, while the portion of the budget devoted to materials fell from 36 percent in 1969 to 28 percent in 1976 (Beazley, 1981). More recently, however, the pattern shifted again: the portion of the budget devoted to staffing fell to 60.2 percent in 1979 while that devoted to materials rose to 30 percent (*Library Statistics*, 1981).

Data beyond 1978–1979 are not yet available from the National Center for Educational Statistics, but data from recent annual reports of the Association of Research Libraries (ARL) indicate that since 1976 there has been a modest change among ARL libraries, with a slightly higher percentage of the budget being devoted to materials in 1981 than in 1976. Whether this trend is continuing among all academic libraries is impossible to determine. Machlup's

(as cited in Cohen and Leeson, 1979) sample of seventy-five academic libraries for the period 1970–1975 was heavily weighted with ARL libraries, and it
showed that the libaries in the sample spent 29.2 percent of their budgets on
materials in 1976 and 60.3 percent on salaries versus the 28 percent and 61
percent noted earlier. An examination of 1981 ARL data shows that the dozen
largest libaries spent 58.6 percent of their budgets on salaries and 30.2 percent
on materials. It may be that the behavior of ARL libraries is slightly different
from other academic libraries, but there is obviously a limit in how far libraries can go in redistributing funds from materials to salaries without departing
from their traditional function of directly providing to their users the materials
on which instruction and scholarship depend.

In any event, the general pattern of the 60–30–10 rule seems to have
been maintained, up to the present, but it also seems inevitable that
accumulating pressures will compel radical changes in the years immediately
ahead. The primary reason for this is the continuing inflation in the cost of
library materials, coupled with the rapid and continuing growth of publications (see King and associates, 1976, for example). Between 1976 and 1981,
the Higher Education Price Index (HEPI) shows an index increase in periodi-
cal and book prices from 251.8 to 400.0 or a total of 148.2, and an average
index increase of 29.66 per year (Research Associates, 1981). In the same
period, the total HEPI index rose from 137.8 to 203.4, considerably less.
Although there is no definitive data on what happened to all academic library
budgets, it is unlikely that they kept up with the HEPI rate of increase.

In fact, the ARL data over the same period show that the number of
serial titles acquired increased by only 1.7 percent per year, while the gross
number of volumes added to the collections actually declined by 3 percent per
year (Association of Research Libraries, 1981). This last statistic conforms the
earlier observations of Machlup and others of the continuing shift within the
acquisitions budget between monographs and serials. In 1970, 62 percent of
the acquisitions budget was spent on books and 34 percent on serials, but, by
1976, 44 percent was spent on books and 50 percent on serials (Cohen, 1979).
At least for ARL libraries, this trend has certainly continued and the rate of
transfer has even accelerated (Association of Research Libraries, 1981). During the years 1975–1981, the average increase in expenditures for serials
among ARL libraries was 13.8 percent per year, while for nonserials, which
includes books, the average increase was 4.8 percent. Neither of these
numbers was enough to maintain past levels of acquisitions, let alone maintain
the fraction of the world's published output that individual libraries were
acquiring in the early 1970s.

These pressures are provoking an excruciating dilemma for academic
librarians. The percentage of the budget provided to libraries is unlikely to be
increased because there is a ceiling, no matter how ill defined, beyond which

institutions will not go in supporting their libraries, since to do so would subvert other institutional purposes. Within the library budget, librarians have been unwilling or unable to increase materials funds enough to offset inflation, so they have done the only thing left: manipulated the components of the acquisitions budget. The rate of growth for monographic acquisition has already turned negative, at least for ARL libraries, and the rate for serials is likely soon to do the same. By the standards of the past, the quality of the collections is rapidly eroding.

Librarians are already being forced to examine whether they can break the constraints of the 60–30–10 rule. Can any portion of the 10 percent devoted to other expenditures be transferred to acquisitions? If expenditure percentages for all academic libraries are similar to ARL libraries, the prospects for doing so are unlikely. "Other expenditures" for ARL libraries are growing faster than any other portion of the total library budget, except serials. Why? Probably because this portion of the budget funds automation. The great hope of the future is automation, not only for increases in productivity but also for resource sharing, since resource sharing depends on communication, which is funded from this part of the budget. To most librarians, it would seem penny-wise and pound-foolish to reduce other operating expenditures. Therefore, significant reductions in this budgetary component are improbable.

The budget for personnel looms larger in the minds of those who seek more funds for acquisitions. As we have seen, the portion of the budget devoted to staffing has, over the past decade, been maintained. (It has only begun to be sacrificed to the acquisitions budget.) This does not mean that changes have not occurred. The number of staff per 1,000 full-time enrolled students declined between 1975 and 1978 (Beazley, 1981), and this decline has probably continued to the present. The net reductions in items acquired may have enabled some libraries to transfer personnel engaged in processing acquisitions to the care of the collection. Since libraries are accretive, they constantly grow. As they grow, more personnel are needed simply to manage the collection. So reductions in needs in one area may have been matched by requirements in another.

Despite efforts to automate library functions, there is not much evidence that this has yet saved any personnel costs (White 1981). Indeed, in the early stages of automation, there is little possibility of savings in personnel. For example, to make the transition to a totally automated catalog that no longer relies on cards demands an enormous investment in record conversion, much of which can only be done manually. The newer circulation systems require that machine-readable labels be attached to each circulating book. Security systems, which most libraries have introduced, require that some kind of magnetic strip or label be attached to the book. All of these developments are recent, and, to be fully effective, each requires an enormous manual effort, an effort that most libraries, for financial reasons, must undertake piecemeal and spread over a long time. So, any expectation that the automation, even of clerical processes, will lead to such immediate gains in productivity that staffing can be reduced is illusory.

Even the automation of such intellectual processes as cataloging will not necessarily lead to gains in productivity and may actually reduce present productivity. Why? Because most catalogs are still card catalogs and the automation that libraries have achieved to date is still greatly influenced by this fact. Any cataloger contemplating a change in a cataloging entry that is still represented in the card catalog by card records that may not have any machine-readable form is bound to consider the consequences of change. If present catalogs were all machine readable, with an interactive authority control file that could automatically make the desired change, the situation would be different, but that is not the case. Changes in card catalogs, even those that are machine produced, still require the laborious removal and replacement of cards. When this process is compounded by the introduction of a new cataloging code, the possibilities for changes that result in declines in productivity are obvious. In general, one may conclude that increases in productivity or savings in personnel attributable to automation are unlikely to occur until some critical level of automation is reached, a level that for most libraries is some distance into the future; if it is reached at all, it will require a substantial initial investment of personnel resources.

Gains in productivity in other typical areas of library personnel such as direct public services are also unlikely. Personnel utilization in public services in libraries is more a function of the hours of coverage than it is of actual demand. The first priority in the public services of most libraries is to maintain as many hours of operation as possible. The level of staffing for any particular function is a secondary goal. For example, most libraries that serve large student populations could use more reference librarians on duty during those hours when demand is heavy, but almost none of them can add all the librarians they can use because they cannot afford to do so. Indeed, for this particular function, the demand in large libraries seems to be so open ended that it might be impossible to satisfy it at any feasible level of staffing. Thus, these libraries staff the reference function at a certain level, and no more, almost regardless of demand. Since public services are primarily staffed to provide coverage, reductions in public service personnel can be made only by reducing coverage or eliminating functions. But all of the functions in public services have been established in response to prior demands, almost always demands related to the use of library materials or to the use of the library as a place to study. Efforts to eliminate public services are likely to lead, therefore, to less use of the library.

An issue related to reduction in service is the substitution of nonprofessional for professional staff. The ratio of professionals to nonprofessionals in libraries is now about 1 to 2 (Association of Research Libraries, 1981; Beazley, 1981). But since professionals are paid, on the average, about twice as much as nonprofessionals, the total salary expense of each group is about the same. This prompts a question about whether nonprofessionals could be substituted for professionals, especially in the reference function. And, again, the decision turns on whether the library wishes to maximize usage or not. Libraries are complex and becoming more so, because sources of information are not only proliferating but also becoming more complex. Even skilled users who wander outside their immediate field need a guide or mediator in order to make maximum use of the collections. In the future, this is likely to be of greater importance than in the past. Not only will information sources become more complex, but users will have to seek resources outside of their own library as well. Skilled professionals will become more, rather than less, necessary to this process. Can the percentage of the library budget devoted to personnel be reduced? Yes, but any immediate reaction will require a reduction in the level or type of service provided. Only as automation in libraries reaches a critical point that permits the total elimination of many processes that are now manual will personnel reductions be possible without reductions in service, and by then other information demands may press the library, which will absorb personnel in other ways.

Still, reductions in service may seem preferable to the continued erosion of library collections, if this were a real choice. But, over the long term, it is not. Libraries need to receive budget increases of at least 18 percent per year (White, 1979) even to maintain the status quo for their acquisitions, let alone restore the deficiencies of the past decade or acquire the items that are being issued in ever-increasing quantities. A rate of increase of 18 percent causes a doubling every four years, and the additional amounts needed to satisfy past levels of expectation would require an even greater rate of present increase than in 1980. Personnel costs, roughly, have been held to the same level of increase as other costs in the institution and even below the HEPI rates for ARL libraries. Therefore, explosive rates of growth for acquisitions would soon overcome any savings that could be obtained from reductions in personnel. If the library budget were frozen, and only acquisitions permitted to grow, in four years acquisitions would consume half of the library budget, and, in less than seven years, acquisitions would consume all of it. No academic institution, not even the very wealthiest, can sustain such rates of growth and, as we have seen, none have attempted to do so. The expectations of the past are impossible to satisfy. No manipulations of a library's current budgetary allocations will enable it to do more than retard the rates of erosion in its collections. Even if some librarians are temporarily successful in increasing monies allocated to the library, if this is merely absorbed in acquisitions, the condition of their libraries will soon revert to what it is now, or worse.

The hard fact is that increases in any substantial component of the library budget that are greater than the general level in the institution cannot long be sustained. Libraries and their institutions seem not to have acknowledged this explicitly (White, 1979) but they have certainly acted in ways that restrain the library budget as a whole within or even below the general institutional rate of increase. This restraint, however, will no longer serve. Institutions and their libraries must directly confront the problem and admit to themselves that they cannot sustain the acquisitions levels of the past. Such an admission and an understanding of its consequences on the part of the user population, especially the faculty, would permit the library to act in more imaginative ways. The emphasis on access over possession has already become acceptable as an idea, but it must become an operating philosophy. If libraries are to remain relevant to the academic enterprise, they must be free to seek workable solutions to the problems that confront them. Within the resources at their disposal, only a different use of the acquisitions budget offers a realistic alternative. Is it really unthinkable to divert a much larger portion of the acquisitions budget to cooperative ventures, such as the Center for Research Libraries or to means and methods that enhance access to information? Or is this really, no matter how repugnant, the only viable option?

If it is the sole option, then at least two things are required: First, librarians must educate their constituencies to the necessity for action; second, librarians must move more rapidly to put into place cooperative resource ventures and electronic means of information delivery. Acceptance of the necessity for swift action on the part of library constituencies would permit librarians to expend the funds to achieve what is needed. In the end, this educational effort may be a greater challenge to librarians than the needed improvements in information delivery.

References

Association of Research Libraries. *ARL Statistics.* Washington, D.C.: Association of Research Libraries, annual reports.

Baumol, W. J., and Marcus, M. *Economics of Academic Libraries.* Washington, D.C.: American Council on Education, 1973.

Beazley, R. M. *Library Statistics of Colleges and Universities: Trends 1968–1977; Summary Data 1977.* Washington, D.C.: National Center for Educational Statistics, 1981.

Bowen, H. R. *The Costs of Higher Education: How Much Do Colleges and Universities Spend Per Student and How Much Should They Spend?* San Francisco: Jossey-Bass, 1980.

Cohen, J., and Leeson, K. W. "Sources and Uses of Funds of Academic Libraries." *Library Trends,* 1979, *28* (1), 25–46.

King, D. W., McDonald, D. D., Roderer, N. K., and Wood, B. L. *Statistical Indicators of Scientific and Technical Communication: 1960–1980.* Vol. 1. Washington, D.C.: National Science Foundation, 1976.

Library Statistics of Colleges and Universities, 1979 Institutional Data. Washington, D.C.: National Center for Education Statistics, 1981.

44

Osburn, C. B. *Academic Research and Library Resources: Changing Patterns in America.* Westport, Conn.: Greenwood Press, 1979.

Research Associates of Washington. *Higher Education Prices and Price Indexes: 1981 Update.* Washington, C.D.: Research Associates, 1981.

Stubbs, K. "University Libraries: Standards and Statistics." *College and Research Libraries,* 1981, *42* (6), 527–538.

White, H. S. "Library Materials Prices and Academic Library Practices: Between Scylla and Charybdis." *Journal of Academic Librarianship,* 1979, *5* (1), 20–23.

Richard J. Talbot is director of libraries at the University of Massachusetts, Amherst.

No longer can the academic community afford to assume that the
development of library collections and information sources
automatically and unobtrusively adapts itself to the
changing needs of scholarship.

Collection Development:
The Link Between Scholarship
and Library Resources

Charles B. Osburn

The least visible, yet most comprehensive and portentous, academic planning that has been at work in higher education consistently during the past few decades is library collection development. It has been so quiet and subtle that its influence heretofore has been marginal, if that. Now, however, both higher education and the management of academic libraries have reached a plateau beyond which the development of library collections and the directions of scholarship must necessarily be considered a coherent enterprise if higher education is to continue contributing to society. No longer can the academic community afford to assume that the development of library collections and information sources is a utility function that automatically and unobtrusively adapts itself to the changing needs of scholarship. It is, on the contrary, an intellectual function underpinning scholarly activity, ensuring its continuity, and infusing it with the stimulus for renewed assessment. But collection development is, at the same time, a function whose limitations will increasingly determine the parameters and quality of scholarship in any individual institution of higher learning and collectively in the nation. This chapter will define collection development, explore its historical relationship to academic scholarship, describe its organization and goals, and examine briefly the environmen-

T. Galvin, B. Lynch (Eds.). *New Directions for Higher Education: Priorities for Academic Libraries*, no. 39.
San Francisco: Jossey-Bass, September 1982.

tal concerns of collection development and their implications for academic planning in the development of higher education.

Definition and Organization

Collection development is the process of decision making that determines how the library's resources in support of research and instruction should develop; which books, journals, and other materials should be part of the library's resources and which should not. Often this process is called "collection management" because it involves budget planning and allocation and the coordination of planning with faculty, administration, other librarians, and frequently with other libraries. Collection development is a continuous series of choices made in the context of a library policy that presumes an understanding of local academic needs, priorities, and goals. Its primary functions are the selection of new materials to be added to the collection, review of collections to determine which materials might be discarded or transferred to storage, allocation of budget among subjects, and review and modification of policy in view of changing needs. Clearly, those responsible for collection development must have an understanding of the processes of scholarship, particularly of scholarly communication. Stueart and Miller (1980) provide a very useful digest of the various functions and concerns of collection development, and Magrill and East (178) analyze the literature.

Organization. The formal organization and size of the library staff dedicated to collection development depends largely upon the nature of the parent institution and its academic programs and upon the size of the total library operation. Usually, collection development is the responsibility of an administrative officer of the library (an assistant director), who delegates authority on a subject basis among a number of librarians with specialized training and interests (bibliographers, curators, subject librarians and branch library heads). These librarians regularly and systematically monitor the current availability of published information sources in a variety of formats and select from among them those that are to be acquired by the library. They also maintain communication with the appropriate academic units to be sure that needs are being met and that planning in the library is informed about trends and projections in the academic units. Most often, academic units are represented in these matters by an individual or a committee whose function is to keep the faculty members in the history department, for example, apprised of problems and opportunities in the library and to help the subject librarian communicate with the entire unit. Often, when library staffing is not adequate to provide appropriate attention to all areas, a faculty member assumes some of the routine of collection development. It is the responsibility of the library director to survey changing institutional priorities and goals, to translate this knowledge into library goals, and to acquire the fiscal resources necessary to support collection development. At least, this is the theory behind the organization; sometimes is works, but more often it does not work well. Collection development works best when it is carried out in a spirit of collaboration among libraries, faculty, and institutional administration.

Policy. Since the percentage of the total current production and availability of library materials that any one library can expect to be able to acquire is always quite small, a policy on the kinds of materials to be selected for the library comes into play as a matter of course. Until relatively recently, a policy on collection development was unwritten in most academic libraries, especially in the larger ones. The plans for developing library resources in support of scholarship have existed primarily in the minds of a few librarians responsible for collection development and in the minds of those few faculty who have consistently demonstrated interest in the library by steadfastly and systematically placing orders for books in their areas of specialization. An obvious implication of this arrangement is that individual predilections often determined priorities and patterns for acquisitions spending and for the development of collections.

However, an increasing number of libraries are beginning to depend on a written policy as a management instrument. A written policy on collection development can serve many purposes, chief among which are to aid in the training of personnel, to enhance communications within the library and between the library and the rest of the institution, to lend rationality to the allocation of funds, to facilitate planning in the library and the institution, and to guide the development of collections in support of scholarship. Collection development is central in library operations, since it generates the workload of processing areas, and it is pivotal in the relationship between library and faculty, since it determines the potential level and quality of resources and services available to the scholar. Consequently, the policy guiding collection development is significant for both the library and the parent institution. A recent example of a comprehensive policy is that of the University of California at Berkeley (Koenig and Dowd, 1980).

Philosophy and Goals. Logic suggests that the appropriate force behind the establishment of policy on library collection development would be the configuration and priorities of academic programs, with collection development functioning as a direct service to and integral part of the academic enterprise. However, as this has not always been the case, an understanding of the historical development of the relationship between academic programs and the library may be useful in understanding the present status of that relationship and in charting its future.

Before World War II, much of the responsibility for the selection of books and journals to be added to the library collection in universities was borne by faculty, with the library director, more often than not, serving in a selecting and coordinating capacity. The rate of publication was not so great then as it is today, the variety of information sources was not so broad, the emphasis of scholarly inquiry tended to be placed most heavily on past events of North American and Western Europe, scholarly inquiry was less tightly meshed with current events, and distinctions between disciplines were clearer. But these conditions were reversed after World War II when the society that emerged from it placed a new and higher value on all kinds of information, a value that derived from the vital role information had played in all aspects of the war, ranging from design of weaponry to the sociological implications of military intelligence. The war had stimulated what has been called since then "the information explosion," which is a misnomer unless an allowance is made for an explosion that has lasted forty years. But it was not an explosion; it was a major societal change that touched the roots of academia and pervaded the operations of academic libraries. We are now in the midst of this change that has been evolving for several decades, in fact, at a crux in the evolution of the relationship between libraries and academic communities. The changing relationship between libraries and academic research since World War II is synthesized by Osburn (1979).

Independence. This evolution has accelerated increasingly since 1945, manifesting itself generally in library, rather than faculty, responsibility for collection development and in the establishment of an organized structure for collection development in libraries that formerly had none. The recent recognition by the library profession of collection development as a specific organized effort requiring specialized personnel in libraries is a reflection of this shift in responsibility as well as of the growing complexity of decision making in collection development. Concomitant with this evolution has been the growing independence of academic libraries, especially research libraries. Independence in this case means planning, staffing, and establishing policy within the library organization, informed by the most superficial knowledge of pertinent activities of the parent institution. This kind of independence, or lack of coordination, has not come about through malevolent intention or a scheme for empire building on the part of library administration, but rather as the result of a sense of security, false as it was, experienced equally on the part of the institution and the library that all was going well, that the heart of the university was pumping its life's blood as effectively in 1980 as it had been in 1950.

Of course, there was a great deal of independence throughout higher education in the era after Sputnik, and it has left its mark on many campuses. In the absence of solid academic planning, departments, colleges, centers, and individuals seemed to be able to behave as independently as funding would allow, and quite often that was considerable. Research in most fields, if not in all fields, became increasingly interdisciplinary and entirely new fields were created through cross-fertilization. Over the years, many of them have continued to subdivide into new, separate areas for scholarly inquiry, each with its own literature; the creation of new bodies of literature did not occasion a decline in production in the parent fields, but rather simply added to existing bodies of literature, making them even larger and more complex. In this environment, which did not encourage and indeed probably discouraged planning, coordination, rationality, and the consequent setting of priorities, the management of library collection development resorted to whatever means were available, usually informally, to inform the process. It was also in this environment that the potential of the imagination and creativity of those libraries who were possessed of an ideal for an academic library collection could most nearly be realized. One of the results is that many extraordinarily strong collections for research have been built throughout the United States, although some in unexpected locations set apart from related materials. Another result, in many cases, is that priorities established for collection development within the libraries often exist independently of parent institutions' priorities as they have begun, empirically, to take shape.

Whatever standards have existed for the evaluation of collections and of collection development have not been helpful in guiding the establishment of policy because they have tended to emphasize quantitative criteria rather than the more difficult qualitative criteria. Quite simply, the value of collections and the performance of collection development traditionally have been measured by the number of volumes in the collection and the number of volumes added. In the context of a good policy and a process to implement it, quantitative standards may be valid, for with those safeguards, bigger is certainly better. But some of the activities encouraged by comparison of numbers, which is an annual tradition (Association of Research Libraries, 1981), have not always been in the best interests of scholarship. Recently, the profession of academic librarianship has demonstrated a growing concern about this attitude, and techniques of collection evaluation, including use and user studies and citation analysis are being explored and tested with greater frequency than ever before. These studies can be useful not only in evaluating the existing collection but even more so in guiding policy on the development of collections, for they can provide lines of insight into the sociology of scholarship. The connection between evaluation and policy is essential.

Costs. In days of adequate funding for higher education a loose connection between the library and the academic community could work, because, for all practical purposes, most needs could be met, whether they were those of the academic programs or those of the library's collection development program. Such days have passed, however; they passed a decade ago and higher education is still struggling to acknowledge appropriately the change in the level and structure of funding, leaving libraries and their collection development policies with unrealizable goals and precious little guidance from the parent institution. The expectations that still exist for service from library collections run very high, and their sources range from every academic program and individual scholar to individuals responsible for collection development in the library.

While funding levels for library acquisitions dropped or stabilized through the past decade, the prices of books and journals escalated at an unprecedented rate each year, constantly eroding the purchasing power of those acquisitions budgets. In fact, the problems of inflation are serious and complex; the prices of books and journals escalated more rapidly than any other higher education cost, except for energy, in the most recent years. Adding to the problem, journal prices inflated at an even faster rate than those of books, while the cost of scientific and technical journals, whose base price was already higher than that of most other kinds of journals, rose even more rapidly than the others. At the same time, the rate of growth in new titles of journals outstripped the publication rate of new books while the entire corpus of scholarly materials was growing rapidly. In many university libraries, this situation was reflected in the acquisitions budgets by a growing proportion of the budget being occupied by serials (subscription publications) and by a growing proportion of the serials expenditures being occupied by science and technology journals. It became clear that the extreme logical conclusion to this trend would be that our libraries would eventually find affordable no books at all and only one journal, a chemistry journal.

To make matters worse, experience showed that efforts to control the monstrous serials problem by cancellation were characterized by cancellation of the least expensive titles, which were replaced very shortly by a greater number of new titles costing far more, title by title, than those cancelled. This scenario is documented in a book-length study (Fry and White, 1976) and in subsequent work of the same researchers. It is complicated, moreover, by a further shift in patterns of collection development — thus in implementation of policy — that has been brought on by the sharp escalation of book and journal prices experienced over the past dozen years. The effort to meet the immediate daily needs of scholarship has detracted from those of anticipating future scholarly need and developing the ideally well-rounded collection. This shift in emphasis has manifested itself in decreased acquisition of older, yet significant, materials as a means to preserve the established acquisition level of current publications. The effects of this change on the development of scholarly resources are considerable, with generally more immediate and specific negative implications for the kinds of scholarship requiring historical perspective. As a result, policy decisions with serious local and national consequence have been and are being made.

Present Status

The convergence of this pattern of economic force with an environment that fostered the unbridled development of collections played havoc with whatever policy, written or not, guided library collection development in universities. It continues to do so. One way of looking at this sitaution as a policy matter is to consider that, whereas the focus of library attention prior to the rapid escalation of prices and production was on the development of collections, the emphasis is directed increasingly to the provision of service. The demand on fiscal resources by daily needs of faculty and students holds an ever-higher priority for collections than does building for future generations of scholars. This is positive insofar as it suggests greater attention on the part of library staff to identified program needs, but it is problematic because it tends toward greater duplication of resources among libraries, irrational development from a regional or national perspective, and a longer-term narrowing of scope and reduction in potential of the collective national resources for research.

Cooperation. Until recently, policy decisions about acquisitions have been made simply in response to the crushing influence of the economic tide. Now it is recognized clearly that no academic library can, independently, provide the full range of library resources in support of research and that the solution to local problems of collection development must be approached in the context of national programs of collection development. A thoughtful and stimulating self-assessment of change experienced in collection development in one major university is provided by Miller (1981). At the national level, the Research Libraries Group is designing the format and procedures for establishment of a conspectus of research collections available in the United States. Now being tested by that group of libraries and other institutions in the Association of Research Libraries, it has the potential to serve as the basis of a comprehensive plan for the development of collections nationally, a plan that will be years in the making. In the meantime, it will be important for learned societies to be kept apprised of the information gathered through this process and to be involved in the planning of the configuration of resources on a large scale. In many respects, questions of national policy on scholarship and information are being addressed, so the academic library profession must have the best advice from the scholarly community in mapping the future.

Preservation. The growth of scholarly publication, manifested largely in the number of books, new journals, and technical reports, and the escalating costs of those materials are environmental considerations for libraries that are probably somewhat evident to the scholarly community. Less evident may be the mounting concern about preservation of those materials now in the process of deterioration, but which are judged of lasting value. It is the role of collection development to determine which of the deteriorating materials are to be preserved and in which format they will best serve scholarship in the future. The task of identifying these materials and taking appropriate action has been delayed so long by the academic library profession that it has become an alarmingly colossal challenge. But it is a challenge that is being met much as the general collection development challenge, which is through cooperative effort among libraries regionally and nationally. Again, questions of national policy are at stake.

Technology. Another environmental concern in collection development stems from the advancement of communications technology, specifically computer and optical-disc technology. Although the implications of these technologies for collection development are great, they may not at first appear self-evident because our picture of library collection development heretofore has been limited to book and booklike materials. However, within the past fifteen years, collection development decisions have begun to include options among formats, the chief alternative to paper being a microform edition of a scholarly title. In some cases, more recently, there has been no option because the title, usually a journal, is available only in microform. The new set of choices presented to library collection development by the advancement of microformat technology now foreshadows the great new dimension of choices that is just beginning to be presented by a broad range of communications technology.

If the past holds any value for an understanding of the future, then it is a safe bet that book-format materials will continue to be published and perhaps that their numbers will even increase during the remainder of this century. But they will constitute a diminishing proportion of the total information sources available for scholarly purposes. Since collection development involves the intellectual organization of this information universe for the purposes of selecting the most relevant sources from among the many and identifying duplicative or overlapping sources, the expanded range of information formats makes the process all the more complex. Certain kinds of information will be more appropriate in one format than in another, and format, in this case, means any kind of delivery system of information, ranging from acquisition of a book or journal to the provision of access to text display on a cathode ray tube. Collection development will have to be guided by policy that concerns itself not only with the book format materials but also with the soures of information generated by new technology. Moreover as cooperative collection development programs are designed regionally and nationally, the computer-driven bibliographic systems serving as the bases of communication will play an ever-greater role in formal collection development policy. Given this set of conditions, the gulf between library collection development and the scholarly community is likely to widen, if the relationship between the two follows past patterns. Rochell (1981) provides an excellent look into the near future, suggesting the range of influence technology will have on library services and goals.

Academic Planning and Library Resources

There is a natural, close relationship between scholarship and library resources that has become obscured by the great quantity of materials to be considered and by the flurry of change in academia during the past two decades. Perhaps this natural relationship simply has been taken from granted. Now, however, that libraries throughout the nation are engaged in planning as they never before have been, and planning is given more serious attention in defining the academic character of each institution of higher learning, the time is ripe to meld the two processes.

Planning. Any valid definition of planning in an organization would have to include the concepts of advance deliberation, system, and design. Deliberation is the key to understanding the subtle dynamics of the system that is an institution of higher learning, while an understanding of the system is the key to the best design for attainment of planning goals. In that connection, it is useful to bear in mind that collection development is intended to be a planning fuction; it is not the amassing of materials, controlled only by budgetary limitations. It has become clear that the goals and methods of scholarship change and that these changes can have implications for the goals and methods of collection development. Moreover, change in the processes of scholarship is expressed tangentially in higher education hiring patterns, in the setting of priorities, and the creation, elimination, and level of maintenance of academic programs, whether instruction or research oriented. These changes must be translated into policy for collection development, and they would be communicated most effectively and meaningfully for all concerned through a mechanism of academic planning.

Influence of Resources. In a consideration of the place of collection development in the future of library service to higher education, it would be misleading to suggest that the influence on planning would have only one direction, that is, going from the institution to the library. Institutions of higher learning will have to come to grips with the fact that, whatever academic planning process may be invoked, it will be influenced in some measure by the practical realities of collection development planning. Otherwise, fiscal resources will be wasted, and academic units and individual scholars without adequate access to an appropriate level of library support will be frustrated. Academic planning—whatever that may mean in each institution—must, more than ever before, consider library resources planning with every change that is contemplated in matters of hiring, the creation or elimination of programs, and the definition of mission and goals.

54

Conclusion

To the extent that creativity and scholarship are dependent upon the kinds of resources that are and will be found in libraries, significant academic planning has been going on in libraries of most colleges and universities for many years. Now such planning is becoming more formalized, and its influence is just beginning to be felt outside the library. As collection development in each individual library becomes part of a larger process for the planning of scholarly resources at the regional and national levels, it is especially critical that it also become a part of the larger process for the planning of academic development within each institution. Only through such collaboration can higher education of the future expect the continued development of library collections commensurate with scholarly needs.

References

Association of Research Libraries. *ARL Statistics, 1980–81. A Compilation of Statistics from the One Hundred and Thirteen Members of the Association of Reserach Libraries.* Washington, D.C.: Association of Research Libraries, 1981.

Fry, B. M., and White, H. W. *Publishers and Libraries: A Study of Scholarly and Research Journals.* Lexington, Mass.: Heath, 1976.

Koenig, D. A., and Dowd, S. *Collection Development Policy Statement.* Berkeley: University of California, 1980.

Magrill, R. M., and East, M. "Collection Development in Large University Libraries." *Advances in Librarianship,* 1978, *8,* 1–54.

Miller, J. G. (Ed.). *Collection Development and Management at Cornell.* A concluding report on activities of the Cornell University libraries' project for collection development and management, July 1979–June 1980, with proposals for future planning. Ithaca, N.Y.: Cornell University Libraries, 1981.

Osburn, C. B. *Academic Research and Library Resources: Changing Patterns in America.* Westport, Conn.: Greenwood Press, 1979.

Rochell, C. C. (Ed.). *An Information Agenda for the 1980s.* Chicago: American Library Association, 1981.

Stueart, R. D., and Miller, G. B. (Eds.). *Collection Development in Libraries: A Treatise.* Greenwich, Conn.: JAI Press, 1980.

Charles B. Osburn is vice-provost for university libraries at the University of Cincinnati.

*In a time of tight budgets, rising demands, and exploding
technology, how can universities and their libraries
supply the information necessary for research?*

Resource Sharing and
the Network Approach

Ward Shaw

There is nothing new about the idea of library networks or resource sharing.
For years, libraries have regularly shared their books and magazines using traditional interlibrary loan. The American Library Association has developed
an interlibrary loan code, specifying the kinds of requests that will be honored,
the format those requests should take, protocols for the sending of materials,
fair treatment of recalcitrant borrowers or libraries, and the like. However, a
number of developments in recent years have greatly increased the importance of resource sharing to libraries and have greatly extended the range of
capabilities that libraries can use to accomplish that sharing. Consequently,
growth and expansion of resource sharing among libraries, with accompanying formalization of library networks, is currently one of the critical areas of
library development and one of the major issues facing library managers.

For many years, librarians believed that the best library was the one
that held the most books. Although there was some recognition that service
was important and that "good" books made better collections than "bad" books,
these considerations were largely advanced by librarians with small collections
and of course were "subjective" — meaning "hard to count." However, in the
past twenty years of so, even the largest libraries have recognized that they
cannot possibly hope to collect all the materials that researchers who use them

T. Galvin, B. Lynch (Eds.). *New Directions for Higher Education: Priorities for Academic Libraries*, no. 39.
San Francisco: Jossey-Bass, September 1982.

will demand and that, even if they could acquire everything demanded, the collections would be too large to organize usefully. As a consequence, if libraries are to meet even normal demands, they must rely on resource sharing as an integral part of their everyday activity.

Goals of Resource Sharing

Before we discuss this any further, we had better be specific about what it is that resource sharing should accomplish. There are three major goals. The first is essentially related to housekeeping functions, and it is to ensure that the same task need not be repeated over and over by different libraries. For example, once a book is cataloged by one library, other libraries ought to be able to use that information to create their own cataloging. The profession has made major progress in this kind of resource sharing. The second goal is to extend the capability of any one library to deliver information to users. Ultimately, any user of any library ought to be able to gain access to any document held by any other library. This is admirable, generally agreed to, and is more or less attainable — provided that the user and the borrowing library are willing to pay the cost in both time and money.

The third goal of resource sharing is that individual libraries ought to be able to reduce the demands on their acquisitions budgets, relying instead on other collections to supply needed items. One copy of an infrequently used journal, for example, ought to adequately serve the users of several libraries, and many journals are very infrequently used. The potential savings here are enormous. The Colorado Alliance of Research Libraries has figured that its seven members could save more than $1 million a year in journal costs alone were they to adopt this approach. However, while this makes tremendous sense to administrators, it makes much less sense to librarians, and even less to faculty for two reasons. First, librarians fear that their budgets will be cut, and, second, access to materials through resource sharing is considerably less convenient than is access through a local collection. Both reasons are well founded. The trouble is that solving the convenience problems of resource sharing is expensive. In the current fiscal climate in universities, such money generally is only likely to come from the existing library budgets, and it is very difficult if not irresponsible to damage what works — local collections — in favor of what might not work as well — resource sharing.

The difficult with that argument is the presumption that local collection building works. It is clearly too expensive for us to continue to rely on local collections alone, and much attention has recently focused on how to improve resource sharing so that it may be of greater help in the library administrator's nearly impossible task of meeting ever-escalating demands with constantly stable or shrinking purchasing power.

Will Rogers once said, "Liberty don't work as well in practice as it does in speeches." The same is true of resource sharing. The basic problem is that it takes time to accomplish the transportation of a particular item from one location to another—time that the researcher may not have or may not be willing to spend. Three elements must be in place for any resource sharing to proceed, and how effective they are governs the usefulness of the approach. First, the libraries involved must agree to arrangements for access and must trust each other to carry them out. Second, there must be a mechanism for determining which libraries hold which items and whether they are available. Third, a mechanism for delivering the material to the user must exist. The effectiveness of resource sharing will depend directly on how good these elements are.

Obviously, manual methods are far too cumbersome. Luckily, technology has advanced to the point that a serious attempt to improve these three essential elements is possible, and indeed much has been accomplished in the past decade. The enabling force has been the development of computer and telecommunications technologies, and the capability they bring to store huge files of information and to search those files from remote locations. Such technology is expensive; although costs are dropping, it is beyond the means of most libraries to conduct major automation projects. Further, and more important, the major benefit of library automation—beyond streamlining internal housekeeping tasks—lies in the sharing of resources among libraries. Librarians have had to invent new agencies—library networks—to administer this strategy.

Library Networks

Library network organizations are of many kinds, ranging from small, informal talking groups to not-for-profit private corporations of considerable size. Different organizational structures work for different kinds and levels of tasks. These networks exist to increase the resources that individual libraries can supply to solve particular problems and to administer common approaches to those problems. Certainly the most successful of the large networks is OCLC, Inc., headquartered in Columbus, Ohio. The network grew out of the concept of shared cataloging; once one of the member libraries catalogs a book, all the other members libraries can use that cataloging. The basic approach was greatly enhanced by the Library of Congress's MARC project, which provides much of the cataloging of that institution in machine-readable form. OCLC takes that information, along with cataloging contributed by its members, and maintains a gigantic data base of cataloging information accessible to each of the members via on-line computer terminals. Thus, it provides a service that meets the first goal of resource sharing—ensuring that tasks once accomplished need not be endlessly repeated—and has saved the member libraries millions of dollars. As a carefully planned by-product, OCLC, Inc., and its approximately 3,000 members have also created a central file of the holdings of those members. This is a major step toward facilitating the sharing of library materials because it provides a quick, accurate, and comprehensive method of discovering what library holds a particular item that may be needed. The shared cataloging activity has been in operation for about a decade, and more recently an interlibrary loan location and requesting function has been successfully operating, significantly reducing the time required to find and request materials.

Other nationwide networks have been successful as well. The Research Libraries Group (RLG) grew out of a computerized library system at Stanford University and counts among its participants many of the largest research libraries and their parent universities. Based on a system of shared cataloging much like that at OCLC, RLG is a partnership directed specifically toward enhancing the nation's research capability and operates a variety of other programs of coordinated acquisition and preservation of material as well as its cataloging program. RLG has made the most concerted attack to date on the third major goal of resource sharing—that of reducing the pressure on acquisition budgets. The Washington [state] Library Network is larger than its name would imply and has made some progress toward providing integrated on-line computer services to libraries.

Many state libraries support library networks of a sort, usually built around the concept of a hierarchy of collections to which to turn for the location and supply of itmes, and often including a payment for a lending program, whereby a lending library is compensated for the costs it incurs in loaning materials. This latter represents an important, albeit insufficient, attempt to deal with a difficult problem associated with resource sharing: It is costly, and unlike building local collections, its costs are transaction sensitive. When a library purchases and catalogs a book, it incurs a certain cost, and the book is then available for as many of its users as wish to use it—up to the point, of course, when it falls apart. Consequently, the interest of the library is served by encouraging as many people as possible to use that book because the bulk of the cost has already been met. On the other hand, when a library acquires the loan of an item from another institution in response to a particular user's demand, there is no leverage. The cost is fixed and associated directly with the single use.

As resource sharing, along with the increasing use of external information services, becomes more important, this economic phenomenon challenges one of the basic rationales of libraries—reduce the cost by spreading the use—and will soon require that libraries look very carefully at their budgeting and costing mechanisms. Rapid changes are now upon us, and it is extremely critical that library administrators develop considerable flexibility and understanding in their budgetary processes.

Regional and local networks, often formed for special purposes, are also an important part of the network scene. They take a variety of forms of governance and organization and are most often controlled directly by the member institutions. Because they are small and locally controlled, they offer the best approach for small, special system research and development and for the construction of specific direct products for homogeneous groups of institutions. It has been mostly at this level that another of the major issues related to resource sharing and networks has emerged.

Libraries, particularly academic libraries, are large bureaucratic organizations, and in many cases are subentities of larger, more bureaucratic organizations — universities. These universities are often state supported and controlled and married to the state government's organization to varying degrees. Large public libraries are almost always creatures of city governments. Library networks and resource-sharing projects, by their nature, cut across institutional boundaries and organization charts. It is often exceedingly difficult to orchestrate the blending of different organizational and bureaucratic styles, rules and regulations, and attitudes that inevitably occur in such a mix. Further, public institutions, especially educational ones, are notoriously short of capital, and in the current economic and political climate that is not likely to change. However, network projects typically require large initial investments of capital funds, usually because they represent change, and change must be proved advantageous before it can be paid for. This usually requires help from the private sector, further compounding the problem of the mix of differing organizations. For example, public institutions cannot usually commit funds for longer than a year, because they ultimately depend on tax revenue. It is therefore difficult to convince a library, for example, to cancel a journal subscription and rely on another institution to acquire the title and make it available when that institution cannot guarantee that it will continue to acquire it. The long-range commitment problem also raises havoc with network's access to credit, because most depend on the member institutions for their assets. Another example is that most public institutions cannot enter long-term joint ventures with private corporations, but that is just what is required to develop many network systems of great potential benefit. Once again, flexibility and understanding are critical.

Assessing Networks

A friend, a network administrator, has a sign on his desk that reads "Cooperation Is An Unnatural Act." During the late 1960s and early 1970s, when the idea of networks was relatively new and money in higher education and libraries was relatively abundant, it was considered the thing to do to join a network. All manner of projects were undertaken, and, predictably, when money became scarce, many of those projects died. The honeymoon period for library networks is over, and it is responsible and necessary for institutions to enter only those network arrangements that provide real and measurable benefit to the institution. Many network projects do provide benefits, but many do not. They key in assessing whether to participate in a particular project, beyond the obvious considerations such as cost or strength of management, is to look for the leverage—for what is to be gained by a consortium approach as compared to an individual one. In the OCLC situation, as we have seen, that leverage was and is twofold: First, libraries could gain the advantage of using other institutions' cataloging, and, second, a spin-off product would be a union catalog of locations of considerable benefit to resource sharing. OCLC has considered, from time to time, offering a capability for a circulation control whereby libraries could perform their housekeeping function of keeping track of lending of material to their users. Unlike the shared cataloging function, this circulation control is clearly not an appropriate network project, at least not at a national level, because there is no leverage. There is little benefit in sharing the information created, because it is specific to each individual institution. Rightly, circulation control has not been successfully implemented at OCLC. Instead, individual libraries and small groups of libraries, often in concert with private vendors, have successfully accomplished it, at less cost and greater benefit.

Technology is advancing rapidly, and the concept of a library is changing—in fact has changed—from a warehouse for books to a center for and mediator of access to information from a variety of sources. Library networks and resource sharing offer a powerful tool to administrators seeking to maximize the research resources for their institutions. Wise administrators will provide their institutions with flexibility, will be prepared to radically shift existing patterns, and will look for leverage. Carefully applied, the network approach can carry the library and the university far beyond what it can do for itself.

Ward Shaw is executive director of the
Colorado Alliance of Research Libraries.

*Continuing disintegration of portions of our research collections
printed on unstable paper threatens our national capacity for
productive scholarship. Effective solutions will require a
heightened awareness of the basic fragility of the modern book
and a coalition of scholars, university administrators, and
librarians committed to cooperative action on a national scale.*

Preservation:
The Forgotten Problem

Patricia Battin

*Preservation of printed matter is, I think, the great forgotton problem
of our age. It has been forgotten, not by specialists and librarians, but,
to a surprising extent, by scholars, men of affairs, and those who use the
materials of civilization.*

With these words, Daniel J. Boorstin, librarian of Congress, opened the Planning Conference for a National Preservation Program convened by the Library
of Congress in 1976 (*A National Preservation Program*, 1980, p. 11). Six years
later, although the issue of the preservation of our intellectual heritage continues to be a leading topic for intensive discussion, conference presentations,
journal articles, and local initiatives among librarians and specialists, a major
program for concerted productive action still eludes us, largely because the
problem continues to be ignored by scholars, men and women of affairs, and
those who use the materials of civilization.

   Successful resolution of the managerial challenge posed by the deterioration of our collections requires an analysis and understanding of the reasons
underlying our inability to achieve effective collective action in halting the
progressive disintegration of our printed records. Technical solutions exist; the

T. Galvin, B. Lynch (Eds.). *New Directions for Higher Education: Priorities for Academic Libraries*, no. 39.
San Francisco: Jossey-Bass, September 1982.

major task is the development of the managerial and financial capacity to mobilize productive strategies on a national scale.

A brief selected bibliography of the extensive and definitive studies on the technical and historical aspects of book preservation is appended to this chapter. The focus here will be a discussion of the mangerial role in organizing programs for effective action.

The troublesome issue of preservation is a revealing paradigm of the changing requirements of research libraries' organization, decision-making processes, and funding necessary to support and maintain in a technological society the kind of vital, effective, nationally decentralized, and accessible research resources to which our nation has been long accustomed. The lingering effects of persistent, but long invalid, mythologies obscure the recognitions necessary to transform considerable expenditures of energy and motion into coordinated effective action. The particular problem of preservation illustrates the paralyzing effects of two widely held myths that appear to prevent effective management solutions to the potential losses of massive amounts of scholarly resources.

Permanence of the Book

The most damaging and pervasive myth hindering effective recognition of the dimensions of the preservation problem arises from our historical perception of the book as a sturdy and indestructible all-purpose medium for recording, disseminating, and storing the text and images assembled by the human mind. In reality, the modern book is a superior means for providing convenient access to recorded wisdom and knowledge but an indescribably poor storage medium. In our society, books occupy a peculiar status. Universally admired by scholars and academic administrators alike as the obligatory sacred cows of academia, our book collections are poorly treated and their continuing existence largely taken for granted. In regard to books, the scholarly community seems to suffer what the advertising industry calls "wear-out" — the overly familiar is eventually overlooked.

Research findings are definitive regarding the optimum conditions for preventive maintenance. The enemies of books are heat, light, dryness, dampness, dirt, and use. It is ironic that the ideal storage conditions for the modern book — a most fragile means of communication highly susceptible to deterioration through both inherent chemical instabilities and the exigencies of normal use — are diametrically opposed to the purposes for which the book was created. Books should be stored in the dark, in temperatures of 50–65 degrees Fahrenheit, with 50 percent humidity, and proper filtering devices to eliminate air pollutants. As Banks (1978, p. 13) has noted, "It is safe to say that the library environment is essentially hostile to all forms of recorded materials."

The movement of American libraries to combine extensive reading facilities requiring bright lighting and elevated temperatures for reader comfort with open stacks housing valuable research collections was apparently based on a widespread refusal to recognize the vulnerability of the book to temperature and humidity variations and the damaging long-term effects of ultraviolet rays. Extensive research has indicated that for every 18 degrees Fahrenheit *decrease* in temperature, the useful life of paper is approximately doubled. While we regularly restrict access to and routinely provide climate controls for our collections of rare books and early manuscripts—all far more durable than books produced during the nineteenth and twentieth centuries—our large research collections, by user demand, are currently governed by policies antithetical to the proper care and preservation of these irreplaceable records.

It is interesting to contrast scholarly attitudes toward library collections and computers. Computers have been commonly reviled, feared, and considered alien by large segments of the scholarly community, yet universities have consistently housed computers in conditions of optimum security and environmental controls. Scholars, albeit with some grumbling, have nonetheless acquiesced to the demands on their instructional and research habits dictated by the internal requirements of computers. We are just possibly beginning to recognize, contrary to the prevailing wisdom, the superior durability, lower aggregate costs, and relative ease of replacement of computers in comparison to books.

Myths of Collective Capacity

The second pervasive myth is the belief that libraries, as separate entities in our society or our universities, can successfully address and resolve in isolation the technical and financial issues necessary to continuing provision of their traditional services to the citizenry. The complexity of the issues, the interlocking nature of the requisite decisions, the magnitude of the costs, and the changing environment created by information technology now demand cooperative national responses to challenges successfully addressed in former times by individual organizations in relatively isolated environments. Because our universities and research libraries have developed historically within the tradition of autonomous institutional structures and because the governance of our library collections has been heavily influenced by proprietary institutional pride, we lack both the internal and the external organizational capacities for effective cooperative action. The persistent perception among scholars and university officers that contemporary social and economic threats to the viability of our research libraries can be effectively redressed by librarians operating in traditional isolation from institutional and social power is perhaps the single most forceful deterrent to effective action.

Significant preservation of our extensive research collections will not be achieved without concerted national, cooperative action, which must involve substantial capital investment, interinstitutional processes to facilitate informed choices essential to the maintenance of our national capacity for research and scholarship, and radical changes in the management of local collections and institutional commitments. Given traditional patterns of institutional organization, it is currently impossible for librarians, within both their institutions and their professional associations, to command the necessary resources, administrative support, and decision-making authority. And yet the myth persists, on all sides, that scholarly information needs in the technological era can be satisfactorily met within the organizational structures of the past. As Nyren reported in *Library Journal:* "Librarians were chided, by a representative of the Mellon Foundation, for their failure to develop a working consensus of strategy on how the problem of preservation should be approached nationally and cooperatively. Mellon funding, he indicated, would wait upon signs of progress in this area" (1982, p. 140).

In this regard, it is perhaps significant that the two libraries with the most active preservation programs are the Library of Congress and the New York Public Library, where library priorities are not in competition with other components of the process of higher education. This competition is further complicated by the present extreme financial pressures on universities, which all too readily encourage the expenditure of limited funds on immediate crises.

Our research library functions have been historically organized to manage the operation of a series of activities flowing from a mutually accepted set of principles within a stable environment. The role of librarians has been largely the management of academic support services within a given set of reasonably stable academic policies and priorities supported by funding equal to the task. In contrast, the average cost of microfilming an individual volume today, including the labor-intensive activities of selection, bibliographic searching, and records maintenance as well as the expenditures for equipment and supplies, ranges from $50 to $60. The major deterrent to an affordable comprehensive program of microfilming bound volumes is the lack of an automatic page-turner. Aside from other decisions complicating the preservation scene, the facts of cost and scope alone invalidate traditional decision-making processes.

The library profession during the past fifteen years has performed a remarkable service in identifying and describing our preservation needs, initiating the necessary technical research, and establishing, at Columbia University, the first educational program for training the required technical and managerial talent. A notable example of these efforts is the recently completed project sponsored by the Association for Research Libraries' Office of Management Studies, which developed a comprehensive self-study program and a series of practical guidelines to encourage and support the establishment of local in-house preservation activities. A brief review of our activities to date, conducted within the context of the prevailing mythology, will perhaps further illustrate the need for the participation and support of university officers and scholars if we are to move beyond the achievements of individual efforts into the realm of cooperative programs on a national scale.

History of Preservation Efforts

Awareness of the loss of our premier research collections through deterioration and decay first became apparent in our largest and oldest research libraries. The implications became unmistakable for newer collections, since the average shelf life of books printed on acid paper is thirty to fifty years, depending upon environmental conditions and intensity of use. Although efforts of the library profession to persuade publishers to adopt the use of alkaline paper have been unsuccessful in the past, new initiatives by the Council on Library Resources' Committee on Book Longevity and the American National Standards Institute are encouraging. So long as the scholarly community continues to accept the poor physical quality of publications through indiscriminate purchase, there is little prospect for substantial reform.

Book collections were traditionally maintained in reasonably good condition through the labor-intensive application of restoration and conservation techniques to individual volumes. It is difficult to determine the precise time when librarians began to comprehend the volume of the preservation need created by the devastating combination of the nineteenth century introduction of acid paper and the twentieth-century publication explosion.

The concern of the library profession was formalized in 1962 when the Association of Research Libraries commissioned Gordon Williams to undertake a study of the problem in American libraries. The disastrous flood in Florence in 1966 served to dramatize the extraordinary vulnerability of our records of civilization and stimulated widespread interest in and renewed awareness of the deplorable condition of our national collections. For example, the Library of Congress has estimated that 30 percent, or six million of a total collection of seventeen million volumes, require some sort of preservation treatment to forestall irretrievable loss. The estimates from the New York Public Library and Columbia University Libraries, which were among the first institutions to establish preservation filming programs, are 50 percent and 30 percent of their respective collections.

The report by Williams (1966) contained the crucial recognition that the massive scale of deterioration had long overtaken our collective capacity to film or otherwise restore all damaged materials and recommended the establishment of a federally supported central agency for selected preservation. A joint conference of the Association of Research Libraries and the Library of Congress held in 1965 continued to exploration of research needs and remedies on a massive scale. In 1972, a study was commissioned by the Association of Research Libraries, funded by the Office of Education, U.S. Department of Health, Education, and Welfare, and conducted by Warren J. Haas to analyze the reasons underlying the failure to implement Williams' recommendations. This study (Haas, 1972) reiterated the need for collective action and proposed the formation of a preservation consortium leading to a national library agency to oversee and coordinate a decentralized national effort. The planning conference convened by the Library of Congress in 1976 again dealt with the recurring themes of the foregoing fifteen years: continuing attention by specialists, the strengthening of isolated local efforts, and little movement toward effective cooperative action.

The Challenge

The lack of response from scholars and university officers to the massive and progressive deterioration in our library collections has confounded the library professions. Faculty resistance to the perceived inconvenience of alternative storage media, such as microformats and the newer optical technologies, has unhappily resulted in unfortunate adversary stances, preventing a cooperative approach to the essential issues. The overwhelming superiority of the convenience of the book as the basic link in the process of scholarly communication has almost totally obscured the necessary recognition of its serious inadequacy as a durable storage medium. Our persistence in continuing to make substantial investments in acid-paper books guaranteed to crumble within fifty years can only be explained by this perverse refusal to concede the fragility of the modern book.

It appears that as a nation we probably cannot mobilize the financial resources required to preserve every deteriorating item in our aggregate collections, even if that were desirable. The selection process will require the participation of both librarians and scholarly specialists to ensure the survival of essential materials. Decisions to permit planned deterioration on a large scale will result in significant changes in the shape and quality of individual institutional collections and influence the ways in which universities will support scholarly research. Cooperative programs imply the pooling and sharing of institutional funds with an accompanying loss of autonomy in decision making.

The kinds of decisions and capital investments required for the preservation of a university's library collection represent long-range planning and budgetary mechanisms that do not commonly exist today in institutions of higher education. Unprecedented economic pressures and severe deferred maintenance crises inherited from prior generations of short-range decision making have created an administrative environment primarily responsive to immediate needs.

The following summary of factors to be considered in planning a successful preservation program illustrates the complexity of the decision process and underscores the need for developing a national collective capacity for action.

1. *International scope of the problem.* In an effort to avoid duplication on an international scale, there is general agreement among librarians that each country should assume responsibility for its own imprints. Understandably, this criterion is troublesome to scholars who have long been accustomed to convenient access to foreign language publications, but it represents at the least a manageable initial attempt to define the scope and assign responsibility.

2. *Separation of the retrospective and prospective problems.* The Library of Congress has taken a bold step into the vacuum of leadership and announced its willingness to accept responsibility for the *prospective* preservation of all American imprints. This action on the part of the Library of Congress will enable other research institutions to manage local collections within the context of the existence of a comprehensive national collection of American imprints. The program, which carries a projected 1983 budget of $7 million includes the application of the diethyl zinc process (developed by the Library of Congress) to neutralize acid-paper publications on a massive scale for approximately $3 to $5 per volume. This process is, of course, applicable only to those materials printed on paper that has not yet deteriorated. The Library of Congress plans to deacidify all future imprints at the time of acquisition. The second major effort involves the development of optical-disk storage capability for newspapers and periodicals.

3. *Organizational structures for the coordination of efforts in our distributed national collections.* Such a program requires consideration of the following components:

- Analysis of collection strengths and conditions of material in our research collections
- Coordinated assignment of institutional responsibilities to ensure filming and storage of master negatives of essential scholarly materials in designated subject areas
- Standardized, computer-supported records to eliminate duplication of effort
- Bibliographic control and access provisions for the scholarly community
- Planning for local collection management within the resulting national context.

One effort, involving twenty-eight libraries, has created an interinstitutional capacity for sharing the costs of collective retrospective preservation activities. The Research Libraries Group, an incorporated partnership of twenty-seven research universities and the New York Public Library, have followed the lead of the Library of Congress and accepted responsibility for filming their collective holdings of American imprints and related Americana published during the years 1876 to 1900, a period when paper of a notoriously poor quality was used by publishers. The selection of institutional holdings to be filmed followed an intensive effort of several years duration to inventory and identify the strengths of member holdings. Appropriately annotated bibliographic records will be entered into the Research Libraries Information Network to provide national access to the master negatives and to prevent subsequent duplication of effort. The corresponding automation of the National Register of Microforms of the Library of Congress will provide a system of comprehensive scholarly access to our retrospective collections in microformat.

4. *Choice of storage format.* Decisions in this area require a choice between the conservation or restoration of the original artifact and the preservation of the intellectual content in another medium, such as reprints or photocopies on acid-free paper, microfilm, microfiche, or digitized storage formats. The range of formats, comparative costs, and convenience of use and storage must all be considered and involve both scholarly and administrative concerns.

5. *Selection process based on scholarly value.* As indicated earlier, the Library of Congress and the Research Libraries Group have made initial decisions based on broad criteria of the country of publication and chronology. These criteria have obviously been selected to facilitate large-scale, easily definable, cost-effective activities in the absence of scholarly involvement in the selection process. Bagnall and Hench (1981, p. 2) have indicated scholarly opposition to filming "chronological slices of material, without regard to importance of field." They urge the learned societies "to help bring scholars together with librarians in major research libraries to develop preservation programs in which the societies supply the expertise to allow informed judgments to be made about what to do first."

Summary

The preservation of our disintegrating paper records presents a series of managerial challenges to librarians, scholars, and university administrators.

1. The relatively infrequent use of retrospective materials blunts widespread recognition of the seriousness of the deterioration and the implications for scholarship.

2. Our traditional library environments are friendly to users and hostile to books. Proper environmental controls for our book collections will significantly raise energy costs and create fundamental changes in scholarly habits and research practices.

3. The labor costs of selection of individual titles require the development of strategies and technologies in support of mass conversion activities.

4. The magnitude of the costs and the sheer volume of materials to be preserved require organizational capacities for collective action demanding institutional commitments rather than the voluntary contributions traditionally characteristic of cooperative efforts among universities and research libraries.

On the local level, environmental controls and use policies should be carefully reviewed to ensure maximum protection and longevity for book collections. In the long run, the installation and maintenance costs of environmental systems are far less than either the intangible costs to the institution incurred through the loss of valuable scholarly resources or the substantive costs for wholesale reproduction in less fragile formats.

At the same time, it must be recognized that, as a society, we have yet to achieve the capacity, within our existing organizational structures, for effective collective action. The primary managerial challenge is to find a way, within our pluralistic society with a strong tradition of institutional individualism, to forge a coalition among the interested parties — scholars, librarians, university officers, publishers, and all those who use the records of civilization — with a common purpose strong enough to transcend the barriers of apathy, tradition, myth, and institutional self-interest. Our national heritage is at stake.

References

Bagnall, R. S., and Hench, J. B. "Technology and the Learned Societies: Microforms, Videodiscs, and Computerized Repertories." Presentation delivered at the American Council of Learned Societies Conference of Secretaries, November 1981, Hamilton, Bermuda.

Banks, P. N. *The Preservation of Library Materials.* Chicago: Newberry Library, 1978.

A National Preservation Program: Proceedings of the Planning Conference. Washington, D.C.: Library of Congress Preservation Office, 1980.

Nyren, K. "News in Review, 1981." *Library Journal,* January 15, 1982, *107* (2), 149-150.

Selected Bibliography

Darling, P. W. "Our Fragile Inheritance: The Challenge of Preserving Library Materials." In *ALA Yearbook.* Vol. 3. Chicago: American Library Association, 1978.

Darling, P. W., and Ogden, S. "From Problems Perceived to Programs in Practice." *Library Resources and Technical Services,* 1981, *25,* 9-29.

Environmental Protection of Books and Related Materials. Library of Congress Preservation Leaflet no. 2. Washington, D.C.: Library of Congress, 1975.

Haas, W. J. *Preparation of Detailed Specifications for a National System for the Preservation of Library Materials.* Washington, D.C.: Bureau of Libraries and Educational Technology, 1972.

Williams, G. R. "The Preservation of Deteriorating Books." *Library Journal,* 1966, *91,* 51-56, 189-194.

70

Patricia Battin is vice-president and university librarian, Columbia University.

The solution to the problems of information overload
and the management of scholarly information lies in productive
use of technology, sharper focus and greater integration in
handling information, and expansion of the roles of academic
library staff.

Professionalism and Productivity: Keys to the Future of Academic Library and Information Services

Millicent D. Abell
Jacqueline M. Coolman

Nothing will be as important to the quality of library and information services provided to scholars and students within colleges and universities as the quality of the people recruited, retrained, retained, and supported to manage and deliver those services in the next two decades. Key to employing people of sufficient caliber to meet the research demands of scholars will be the vision and commitment of academic administrators, including library directors, to the restructuring of library and information services within their respective institutions. The vitality of the scholarly information system is at stake. Traditional means of making recorded knowledge available must be reinforced and reinvigorated; new means of data exchange must be employed. All such efforts must be related systematically to make effective utilization of recorded knowledge and data.

Elsewhere in this book numerous factors contributing to the problems and prospects for academic libraries are identified. Among the most important are the persistent labor-intensity of library operations; the growth and spread

T. Galvin, B. Lynch (Eds.). *New Directions for Higher Education: Priorities for Academic Libraries*, no. 39.
San Francisco: Jossey-Bass, September 1982.

of computing and communications technology applied to information generation, storage, and transfer, as well as to conventional library operations; and
the continuing expansion of recorded information coupled with ever-increasing scholarly information needs.

Many of these factors call for an expanded service role for the academic
library at a time when all of higher education is experiencing intense fiscal
pressures. The question is, how do we do more with less? The answer lies, in
large part, in better utilization of the library's human resources through
improved productivity and a reinterpreted professional role for librarians, a
role more appropriate to scholarly requirements and technological opportunities and, hence, even more demanding than it is today.

The Current Scene

With few exceptions, such as the student worker who checks out books
or the staff member at the reference desk who helps to track down an elusive
citation, library staff are all but invisible to library users. Yet libraries are
highly labor-intensive operations. In 1980–1981, $517,741,432 — 56 percent of
the aggregate budgets of the 113 members of the Association of Research
Libraries — were expended on personnel (Association of Research Libraries,
1981). Despite their substantial personnel costs, most academic libraries are
inadequately staffed to provide service of the quality or extent appropriate to
support the academic mission of the university.

There are several possible explanations for the inability of academic
libraries to provide fuller service given their staffing resources. First, librarianship is a complex and extensive enterprise that requires its practitioners to
maintain awareness of the ever-changing universe of information resources as
well as dynamic segments of the local library collections. Librarians must also
anticipate user needs, seek materials or information in various forms from
myriad sources, and organize materials and information in coherent systems
from which they can be retrieved. In addition, they must maintain awareness
of current developments in scholarship, technology, and management; exer-
cise influence on the producers of information to try to establish accessibility
and standards of quality; cooperate with each other to ensure maximum availability of publications and information; be active politically to protect the free
flow of information, sometimes threatened by government policies; and the
like.

Second, partly because of the complexity of developing appropriate
software and partly because of the substantial size of the initial investment in
automation for large academic libraries, many libraries are still dependent
upon manual systems for routine operations. A sense of the scope of this problem is conveyed by data collected during 1981–1982 by the library of the

University of California, San Diego, a middle-sized library in the Association of Research Libraries group. It was determined that implementation of full-scale automation of basic library operations would eliminate the handling of over three million pieces of paper per year and release a significant number of staff for the other purposes.

The invisibility or undervaluing of library staff may diminish the effectiveness of the library in providing access to information, or it can, through conscious effort by librarians and administrators, be turned around to ensure that the potential for library and information expertise is more broadly recognized and exploited on behalf of researchers, teachers, and students.

Staffing Patterns. Contemporary academic libraries have three principal staff groupings. The least numerous staff group is that of the professional, the librarian. Typically, the librarian holds at least one advanced degree, the master's degree in librarianship or information science. Librarians are generally charged with leadership roles within libraries, predominate in library administration, and hold almost all key positions in departments and branches. In addition, librarians serve as the principal liaison with faculty in determining collection and service needs, provide a range of reference and instructional services, make decisions with regard to acquisitions and collection management, and provide leadership for cataloging activities.

The daily operations of libraries, which entail considerable supervisory responsibilities and the performance of myriad, highly complex tasks, are largely handled by a group of support staff, variously denoted and deployed, who range from paraprofessional to clerical in duties, skills, and titles.

The third group of workers, one on which academic libraries are heavily dependent, is the corps of student workers. This is probably the group most visible to library users. They typically perform tasks that do not require extensive training, such as the checking out and shelving of books, monitoring of exits, and the like.

Changing Nature of Staffing Patterns. Our description of the staff reflects the changing nature of staffing patterns and changing expectations for staff in academic libraries in recent times. Starting at the top, there is considerable evidence that, in spite of some strong faculty sentiment to the contrary, academic administrators are increasingly seeking and appointing to library directorships persons with proven leadership and management abilities in academic libraries in preference to the scholar-bibliophile who often lacks the requisite administrative skills. Among the rank-and-file librarians, one can discern a trend toward more rigor in the advancement and promotion process, with greater emphasis on professional contribution and development than has existed in the past. Demands placed upon the professionals are greater; academic librarians are increasingly liberating themselves from a nine-to-five task orientation, and they are recognizing and fulfilling roles of leadership and essential interaction with peers, clients, and vendors. The support staff has, in turn, steadily assumed greater responsibility for many library operational tasks, including most acquisitions and circulation functions and the majority of cataloging functions.

A significant challenge to the professional remains. In the dynamic process of change and growth in roles, the support staff's gain may have been greater and more rapid than that of librarians. As Veaner (1982, p. 12) asked:

> Yesterday's librarians did a lot of work that is now routinely done by library assistants. The librarians who entered our profession twenty years ago, or even ten years ago, brought with them career expectations that perhaps can no longer be delivered by society and its institutions... [Library support staff] now perform very complex work functions; their work has risen in sophistication. Has the work of librarians risen correspondingly in professional character and discipline?

Building on the growing sophistication of library staff and responding to anticipated requirements, the upgrading of library personnel capabilities must continue and indeed, accelerate through conscious and focused efforts. As noted by Smith (1982, p. 1): "We recognize that major changes are occurring and must continue to occur with regard to the overall quality of research library staff, how each staff category is utilized, and how the total staff is most effectively and efficiently deployed within the library." To provide a framework within which the impetus for these changes and likely requirements can be addressed, as well as some notions with regard to possible patterns in the 1990s, we offer some propositions regarding future library staffing here.

Proposition One. Changes in the character of the nation's labor force will be evident in the work force of academic libraries.

During the next decade, radical changes occurring in the nation's work force will have an impact on academic libraries. Among the more striking changes identified by scholars, researchers, and demographers are the unparalleled growth in the size of the labor pool, the increasing cultural and ethnic diversity of that pool, the changing attitudes of workers toward their work, and the rising educational level of workers.

Growth of the labor force. During the 1980s there will be a dramatic increase in the number of prime-age workers. This trend will reach its peak about 1990, when the entire "baby boom" generation — those born between 1946 and 1964 who now comprise one-third of the nation's population — will be concentrated between the ages of twenty-five and forty-four. Freeman (1979, p. 75) notes that this bulge in the prime-age work force is unprecedented and problematical:

Whereas in 1975 there were 39 million workers in the 25–44 bracket, in 1990 there will be 60.5 million — an extraordinary 55 percent increase. . . . This remarkable age bunching of the work force will have far-reaching consequences for the job market. . . . It suggests fierce competition for promotions, coupled with substantial career disappointment for many and the possibility that persons in the 25–44 cohort of 1990. . . will receive especially low relative income for their entire lives.

Although, on the surface, libraries would appear to benefit from the growth of the labor force by becoming increasingly selective in their choice of employees from among those available, there will be considerable competition for the services of the most highly qualified individuals from other sectors of the economy. Secondly, because the bulging work force will restrict opportunities for mobility, there is a potential for significant employee morale problems.

Diversity in the work force. The work force of the next decade will include increasing numbers of women and minorities. While the nation's work force as a whole will include more diversity, academic libraries will have to continue to engage actively in affirmative action efforts to attract minority workers. As noted by Porat (1976), the participation of blacks and other racial minorities in the information sector of the economy is quite small, and their share of high paying jobs is almost nil. He observes further that, although women tend to predominate in the information work force relative to men, their tasks are generally less prestigious, more routine, less career oriented and less lucrative. Academic administrators must ensure equal opportunities for advancement and participation in higher paying jobs within libraries.

Changing attitudes toward work. As reported by Yankelovich and others, the presence of the baby boom generation in the work force will require that a different set of motivational incentives be employed by management. As Yankelovich (1979, p. 3) put it: "A New Breed of Americans, born out of the social movements of the sixties and grown to majority proportions in the seventies, holds a set of values and beliefs so markedly different from the traditional outlook that they promise to transform the character of work in America." Yankelovich's analysis of the values and beliefs that "new breed" workers bring to the work place indicates that the shaping force underlying their ethic is the preoccupation with self, which flourished in the 1960s and 1970s. He suggests that this emphasis on the self, when brought to the work place, translates into an expectation that work will provide an opportunity for self-expression and self-fulfillment, and that the employer will demonstrate a significant interest in the employee as a person with needs, talents, and rights.

Younger employees increasingly question traditional definitions of success and are more inclined than their elders to forego monetary compensation for rewards intrinsic to the work itself. They are also less willing to subordinate their personalities to the work role. Therefore, to ensure a more satisfying and productive work environment, incentive systems must be diverse enough to suit the desires of the various individuals in the work force. Moreover, according to Yankelovich (1979, p. 24): "For a large minority (about 35 percent of the work force), particularly the better educated, the substance of the work itself must be inherently interesting and challenging." Although many persons are now attracted to librarianship because the work itself can be interesting, too often library jobs are stultifying. It is imperative, especially if more highly qualified people are to be attracted to and retained in libraries, that flexible incentive systems and challenging assignments be provided.

Rising educational level. The new generation of workers is, on the whole, better educated than any of its predecessors. The better-educated workers are those most interested in obtaining jobs that provide opportunities for the use of their abilities and for self-expression, as well as traditional economic and material rewards. They also, increasingly, demand a voice in decision making regarding their work. The demand for more participation in decision making represents a threat to some conventional patterns of decision making. The dilemma for management is that the claim to a legitimate and meaningful role in decisions is much more difficult to satisfy than are direct economic demands, which are tangible and present few threats to existing organizational structures. Regardless of this difficulty, the issues that academic libraries confront are so complex and the need for specialized knowledge is so great that there will, necessarily, be a continuing trend toward distributed and shared decision making.

Proposition Two: *Academic institutions are presented with new opportunities by the radical changes in computing and communications technologies and will require modified organization, a new melding of skills within the institution and among organizations, and a more active role for libraries to take advantage of these opportunities.*

The new technologies promise powerful and convenient means for the manipulation and exchange of information. They range from high-density, random-access data storage devices, such as the optical disk, to electronic mail and satellite teleconferences. Scholars in virtually every discipline are taking advantage of these technologies, if only for word processing.

For many purposes, individuals and institutions are moving toward decentralized access and decentralized computing. Concurrently, sources of electronic data from individuals and from scholarly and commercial publishers are proliferating. With the increasingly easy availability of information, individuals will command greater amounts of information directly, by terminal in the office or at home. However, there is a danger that individual scholars and institutions will be overwhelmed both by choices of data sources and by technological choices, often involving substantial investment in essential but obsolescent systems.

Academic institutions must reconsider the organization of their information functions if they are to make optimum use of the results of internal and external ingenuity and entrepreneurship. Consideration must be given to the option of capitalizing on the capabilities of academic libraries to facilitate access to information in electronic form. At the Academic Libraries Frontiers Conference sponsored by the Council on Library Resources in December 1981, Steven Muller, president of Johns Hopkins University, proposed a closer organizational link among campus information systems, both traditional and electronically based, under the organizational umbrella of the library. The rationale for such a linkage is that the foundations of librarianship lie in the organization and retrieval of information. If librarians are to achieve greater effectiveness in helping with the adoption of new technologies, both a recognition of the relevance of librarians' educational background and experience and an upgrading of their abilities to interpret and exploit these technologies are required.

Certainly, many of the traditional functions of the academic library will persist. Existing collections are unlikely to be replaced by alternative media except as a means of preservation. Books will continue to be valued as usable sources of knowledge, ideas, and information. Books in specially focused collections will continue to be invaluable to scholarship. Libraries must not devalue their responsibilities to maintain and provide access to these book collections.

In addition, however, as Birdsall (1982) suggests, librarians should be concerned with facilitating direct access to information, through creation of needed techniques and services. Helping to identify and discriminate among information sources, assisting in the design of local information systems, and participating in the planning of information networks are all possibilities for an expanded role for the librarians to meet the needs of the institutions and clientele with which they are associated.

Compounding the institution's and scholar's difficulty in managing information is the increasing activity of the private sector in the provision of electronic information. It is essential that deliberate efforts be made to ensure that information products meet the needs of scholars. It is therefore essential that scholars (as producers and as consumers of information), publishers (both scholarly and commerical, print and electronic), and librarians work closely together to guarantee that a viable market and distribution system be established with minimal barriers to the free flow of scholarly information.

A range of choices exists for academic institutions and their libraries in meeting the needs and opportunities of the electronic information age. If the library remains in a relatively passive role, there is an increasing risk that access to information will become splintered, chaotic, and wasteful and that the library and librarians will become increasingly irrelevant to scholars' information needs. If an effort is made to capitalize on the existing and potential capacities of libraries and librarians, it may well be possible to avoid waste, thereby enhancing the productivity of the scholarly enterprise.

Proposition Three. *Academic librarianship will become an increasingly specialized profession with scholarly and technical tracks, more selective recruitment, more rigorous professional training, graduate education to supplement the professional degree, and greater emphasis on research. In addition, retraining and continuing education and development for all staff must be recognized as basic necessities.*

The work of librarians in a "technical track" centers on the design and management of systems (often computer-based) for the ordering, cataloging, indexing, and maintenance of book collections, journals, and other library materials. In contrast, the work of librarians in a "scholarly track" centers on the selection of books and other library materials (often within a single or a group of closely related disciplines) and the provision of bibliographic, reference, information, and instructional services to students and scholars. Some of the other particular responsibilities, present and future, of academic librarians are noted elsewhere in this chapter. Generalizations about distinctive continuing and evolving roles for librarians, the kinds of people who should fill these roles, and their qualities and preparation are sources in increasing debate within the profession. Certainly one view that is likely to persist is that of the librarian as intellectual. Isaacson (1982) has commented on the intellecutal foundations and essentially intellectual nature of the work of librarians. He notes that not only intellectual interests but also intellectual judgments are required in librarianship. Further, Isaacson, Martin (1981), and others have noted that the humanistic intellectual traditions of librarianship must be brought increasingly into partnership with scientific requirements of electronically based information systems and the research required to develop more effective and efficient modes of delivering information and of managing the library as an organization. Another requirement, related to these, is the ability of the librarian to facilitate and guide the rapid changes that are occurring in systems of organizing knowledge and distributing information. People with qualities and educational experiences not traditionally associated with librarianship must be found to assume this kind of responsibility.

There are numerous ways to conceive of the possible distinctions among academic librarians of the year 2000. One possibility, admittedly highly speculative, is that suggested by Warren J. Haas, president of the Council on Library Resources, who views academic librarianship as an aggregate of professions, in which all practitioners share an educational grounding in research librarianship. He proposes that the great majority of professionals "should have substantial and active skill and interest in a subject field" and that another 10 or 15 percent should be trained in computer and communications technology, with the balance of the professionals, a small number, specifically trained in and for management (Haas, 1980, p. 20).

These thoughts lead to a consideration of the personal qualities and skills required of a person entering the professional practice of academic librarianship. Of course, the spokespersons for the profession agree that the "best and brightest" must be sought. Somewhat more specificity was lent to this notion by Battin (1982, p. 3) in enumerating four critical qualifications:

1. A first-rate mind with problem-solving abilities.
2. A solid undergraduate preparation in any of a variety of disciplines: the key is the rigor of the training.
3. Concrete evidence of managerial abilities: Almost every research library responsibility, even at the entry level, now requires some degree of sophisticated management of either people or resources.
4. An intellectual commitment to research librarianship.

Other personal qualities, briefly noted here but highly prized, include flexibility, assertiveness, skill in human interaction, tolerance for ambiguity, mathematical and analytical abilities, and willingness to take risks.

Concerns regarding the personal and general education requirements of librarians, as well as the content of their professional education are currently the focus of special attention. At the national level, the Association of Research Libraries (ARL) and the Council on Library Resources (CLR) have launched efforts to address these concerns.

ARL has formed two subgroups to deal with education and with staffing. The Task Force on Library Education was founded in 1980 and works closely with the CLR project advisory group (described later). Their efforts extended into recruitment to the profession, as well as education. In February of 1982, an ad hoc Task Force on Research Library Staffing was appointed to identify the nature, roles, and configuration of staff that will be required in academic research libraries in the next decade.

The Council on Library Resources has raised over $1 million dollars from private-sector sources to develop a program called Professional Education and Training for Research Librarianship. The advisory committee includes representatives from research libraries, library education, and academic administration. As described by Haas (1980), one of CLR's aims is to attract a greater number of exceptional people to research librarianship. Some would be recruited directly from undergraduate programs and others would be people who hold doctorates in a subject field. A second aim is to work with a few first-rate library schools to develop professional degree programs specifically geared to research librarianship. A third component of the CLR program is to support the development of opportunities for internship as an integral part of professional education. A fourth aim is to continue and expand mid-career development programs, for both middle and senior library managers.

Finally, the CLR is concerned with supporting thoughtful consideration of the frontiers of research librarianship through a series of conferences. As Haas (1980, p. 20) states:

> If the profession itself is in a state of transition and research libraries are in the process of making change, not enough attention is being given to the research library operations and the relationships of those libraries to scholarship and all of the other activities related to scholarly communication. We also intend to find ways to support first-rate people doing research and analytical work, in library schools and other parts of universities and in libraries, on a large number of topics, possibly those developed out of the frontier conferences.

The papers and discussions of the first frontiers conference, held in December 1981, will be reported in late 1982 in a book prepared by Robert Hayes, dean of the graduate school of Library and Information Science at the University of California, Los Angeles.

The research required to provide more effective library and information services must take many forms. The likelihood of practicing librarians' conducting such research was cast in some doubt by the participants in a recent Delphi study leading to predictions regarding the academic public-service librarian in the year 2000 (Otto, 1982). The participants viewed the inclusion of research as a major activity of such librarians as desirable but improbable. In our view, librarians must be trained and supported in the conduct of both research and operations analysis. Academic libraries cannot productively and effectively fulfill either traditional or new roles unless there is continuing rigorous questioning of assumptions and examination of practice. Information seeking and use are at least as important topics for study as are technical problems of library operations.

Concurrent with the expression of concern regarding recruitment to the profession, professional education, and research, certain patterns in hiring practices by academic libraries are becoming apparent. The requirement of a graduate degree beyond the master's degree in librarianship is an explicit requirement in filling many academic library positions and is an implicit aspect of recruitment in filling still others. Otto (1982) reported that the Delphi study participants agreed that a subject master's degree, in addition to the professional degree, would be a regular requirement for appointment to a public-service position in an academic library by the end of this century.

Several graduate programs in librarianship have already been strengthened by the addition of specialized programs, internships, joint-degree graduate programs, and a greater emphasis on research.

In contrast to these initiatives to strengthen academic librarianship is the 1982 proposal by the U.S. Office of Personnel Management to reduce academic requirements for federal librarians, an action vigorously opposed by the American Library Association, whose members recognized that such a move by the federal government would exacerbate the potential for lowered education requirements (in the name of cost-cutting measures) for positions in local and state publicly supported libraries.

Much of the preceding discussion relates to concerns about the future practitioners of librarianship. However, some greater though must be invested in the problem of retraining, which is too extensive to be addressed only through ad hoc and unsystematic continuing education programs. Preliminary results from a recent analysis (Fretwell, 1982) of the professional staff of the ARL member libraries indicate that as many as half may have less than eleven years of professional service. Thus a substantial number of current practitioners may well be in place for another twenty or thirty years. Given the radical and rapid pace of change in the conditions and demands that academic librarians confront, it is essential that thoughtful and rigorous programs be developed to help these active professionals maintain effective and relevant skills.

By the same token the library support staff must have opportunities to learn the new skills, supervisory and technical, that the shifting roles within academic libraries require of them. Regardless of current fiscal crises, academic institutions cannot afford to reduce the level of investment in training programs for staff that current conditions require, nor to ignore the quality and efficiency of staff so crucial to the effectiveness and productivity of the institution in its programs of research and instruction.

Proposition Four. *To attract and retain the highly educated and trained personnel needed to staff academic libraries in the years ahead, higher salaries will be required.*

It is widely recognized that about half of this nation's gross national product is in the "knowledge industries," involving the creation, manipulation, packaging, and distribution of information, as well as providing access to it. Even with the growth in the labor pool noted earlier, intense competition for talented personnel, already obvious in the systems and information science fields, is likely to persist. Academic institutions find themselves in serious competition with private industry for knowledge workers, partly because of the growing importance of technology and partly because of the recognition of information as a major commercial commodity.

Academic libraries are not winning the contest. Schools of library and information science report that many of their best students are being attracted by corporations. Certainly, the private-sector salaries are distinctly more attractive. Partly, this reflects the known salary differential between academe and the private sector. In addition, the differential reflects the positive image and rewards associated with information industries in contrast to academic librarianship. The latter often suffers from a stereotypical reputation for dullness, as well as the feminization of the profession. As is typical in female-dominated professions, academic librarians receive relatively lower salaries in relation to male-dominated professions requiring similar educational preparation. Evidence of this appears in the results of recent salary surveys (*American Libraries,* 1981). Graduates of the University of Pittsburgh with the bachelor's degree in information science in 1981 reported an average starting salary of $19,217 for their jobs as programmers, systems analysts, market research associates, and manufacturing engineers. In contrast, the average starting salary for holders of the master of library science degree in 1980 was $14,233.

Another factor contributing to the inability of academe to attract the best recruits is that entry-level jobs are perceived to be, and often are, uninteresting and unchallenging. This is a problem that all academic librarians must be willing to address and solve if they are to attract and retain colleagues of the quality required to ensure vitality of the scholarly information system.

As formats of recorded knowledge and modes of information transfer proliferate, the role of the librarian in the academic setting will continue its expansion from that of keeper and disseminator of printed sources of information to that of broker, interpreter, selector, and packager of information in its myriad forms. This expanding role for librarians will assume even greater importance in the years ahead as members of the academic community find that new and faster modes of access to data tend, ironically, to exacerbate the already serious problem of information overload. To be prepared to function effectively in the new, more complicated academic and research library environment, the librarian must possess an excellent undergraduate education; professional education in the theories, principles, and practices of academic librarianship; thorough familiarity with the spectrum of modes of information transfer, from the most traditional to the most modern; and graduate preparation in a subject or technical field. To ensure the librarian's continued effectiveness, commitment to on-going enhancement of knowledge and skills in all these areas will be mandatory. To recruit and retain individuals of this caliber, academic institutions must be prepared to compete in the open market with private industry and other research organizations.

Thus, the librarians who staff the nation's academic libraries in the years to come will be individually more expensive, even if the cost of compensating them more competitively must be supported by a reduction in their number. Incentives need to be established in addition to higher salaries. The rewards for persons opting for academic careers can be great. As Veaner (1982, p. 19) states the prospect:

We must get across the message that librarianship is not a sinecure for people who "love to read," that librarianship is an exciting and difficult challenge, that we are entering a new age of information science, that we intend to lead in the information business. . . . Library science is a *process,* an evolution, a development. . . an open-ended series of challenges, opportunities and responsibilities.

Concurrently with the shift of responsibilities to support staff and the introduction of automation, as noted in the next section, salaries of support staff members must be reexamined to ensure that they are equitable and competitive with nonlibrary positions requiring like qualifications and making similar demands. It is not always fully recognized that there is an interesting and challenging career ladder within libraries for those staff who are not librarians. Too often the unique character of library work is not fully comprehended by campus personnel offices. The issue sometimes is confused when library workers are classed in an inappropriate clerical series or an inflexible civil service system. Nevertheless, positions that often require multilingual abilities, familiarity with computer-based systems, major supervisory responsibility, and command of a substantial body of knowledge must be properly valued and compensated if libraries are to make those productivity gains needed to served their clientele effectively within their limited resources.

Proposition Five. Intensified information demands, budget stringencies, and increasing adoption of automated systems will result in further changes in library staffing patterns.

Library literature is rife with observations regarding the radical changes occurring or pending within academic libraries, yet that awareness seems not yet to have penetrated deeply into the library user community. As Columbia University vice-president and librarian Patricia Battin (1982, p. 1) said in an address to a group of library educators: "In a sense, the revolution that is rocking research libraries is almost totally obscured to our colleagues by our location in the midst of institutions still largely governed by centuries' old traditions, rituals, and decision-making processes. We live side by side in the same community but in radically different worlds."

There is little question but that academic libraries must be transformed if their institutions are to have effective and productive scholarly information systems, exploiting fully the massive capital investment that has been made in the nation's academic and research libraries. Among the factors to be considered in thinking about how this transformation might lead to altered library staffing patterns are library use patterns, budget stringencies and growing demands, applications of technology within the library, applications of information technology outside the library, the need for greater productivity, and the requirement for greater professional capacity within the library.

Library use patterns. Most information about library use and about information seeking indicates that the patterns differ from discipline to discipline and even between subdisciplines. Hence, a major shift in library services from an emphasis on a collection of printed materials to the establishment of a fully automated data center might be most welcome to many engineers but anathema to classical historians. More thought needs to be given to the organization of library staff in relation to particular clientele groups.

Budget stringencies and growing demands. Dwindling resources in relation to growing demands and the potential for greater information overload make it imperative that librarians engage in close liaison with faculty in determining collection and service needs. Librarians must work closely with faculty in helping to locate and discriminate among sources of information, in building information systems, and the like. The traditional notion of a wholly comprehensive library has been destroyed by compounding budgetary limitations. Today and in the future, the vitality of scholarly information systems depends upon forging a new mix of media and services within budgetary constraints.

Applications of technology within the library. The changes wrought in academic libraries during the past decade by the adoption of nationwide automated systems for cataloging support and literature citation searching will certainly become more pronounced in the years ahead. As automated systems become more fully integrated into conventional library operations, opportunities for redeployment of staff and for improvement of traditional services will appear. For example, acquisitions and cataloging functions will be affected significantly. Because original cataloging is increasingly available through cooperative networks and shared through automated systems, fewer librarians will be needed for such work in the local academic library. As card catalogs are replaced by terminals for public on-line access and as other internal control files are automated, fewer support staff will be required for the maintenance of these files.

To date, with the exception of greater sharing of original cataloging, most library experience with automation has affected clerical functions. There has been little visible effect on the role of reference librarians, other than greater utilization of on-line data-base searching as intermediaries on behalf of clients.

Applications of information technology outside the library. It is obvious that a rapid and profound change in individuals' access to information is occurring. No longer will the ordinary information seeker be dependent on an expert to handle the terminal and manipulate the search strategy in using an electronic data base. Leonard (1982, p. 95) notes three factors that are contributing to this change:

1. Increasing availability of relatively low-cost personal computers with associated software;

2. an increasing number of data communications networks available to the personal computer owner; and

3. changing marketing strategies within the publishing field.

The expansion of the private sector into electronic information distribution places powerful tools in the hands of individuals who have the knowledge and resources to manipulate them. Of concern to academic librarians and their institutions and clientele must be the ability to deliver relevant information of high quality from these systems; to ensure access to information for those persons who cannot pay for direct access themselves; to provide some coherence within and among systems to guard against redundancy and waste; to protect the concept of recorded knowledge and the library's responsibility for its preservation in usable forms (as distinct from the operations of data transfer); and numerous other issues, many not yet perceived.

Need for greater library productivity. Most academic libraries are currently struggling to meet increases in demands for traditional services with few, if any, increases in staff resources. Indeed, many libraries have experienced staffing reductions within the past decade, and hard times lie ahead. This fact, coupled with the ever-increasing demands emerging from the information revolution, makes increases in library productivity imperative if a total breakdown in service is to be avoided. Two means are suggested here for the improvement of productivity. First, the investment, no matter how difficult, in massive automation of internal library operations is required. Until libraries can get their traditional manual operations and files under automated control, it will be impossible for them to assume the leadership so badly needed in the implementation of innovative information functions.

One of the effects of the investment in library automation will be the release of numerous support staff positions. As these positions are released from manual operations, local conditions and the current and future implications for the application of technology must be considered in determining their future utilization. A productive use would be the redeployment of staff and staff dollars to meet the increased work load and the demand for new services that will undoubtedly be generated by the improved operations made possible by automation. Second, productivity can be improved by expansion of the professional capacities of the librarians in their scholarly, technical, and managerial roles. In any case, much work is needed in the development and application of relevant measures of productivity.

Requirement for greater professional capacities. As noted throughout this chapter, it is essential that the professional capacities of the librarian be expanded and enlarged, Academic administrators and faculty must assist librarians in this effort. Capital investment must be forthcoming, salary and classification structures must be altered, entrenched practices and patterns within academic institutions and their libraries must be reexamined and modified, taking risks must be encouraged, improvements in the recruitment and educational preparation of librarians must be made, jobs must be redefined, and the attitudes of librarians and their clientele must change.

One possible scenario for change in library staffing patterns would incorporate a reorientation of the library from its current predominantly functional organizational pattern — acquisitions, cataloging, circulation, and reference — to an organization that is more directly related to broad disciplinary groupings — arts, humanities, social sciences, and physical and biological sciences, depending on the level of specialization appropriate to the particular institution. The librarians acting as liaisons to these disciplinary groups would work with their faculty colleagues in defining information needs and meeting those needs. They would be assisted by their colleagues with computing and communications skills in creating and adapting technology appropriate to local or shared needs. Support staff of considerable expertise would manage internal automated operations and a variety of sophisticated established services. The entire enterprise would be administered by persons educated and skilled in librarianship, information science, and management and capable of organizing the efforts of specialists in order to provide systems and services more powerfully and flexibly than they could provide working independently.

Conclusion

It is important to distinguish those influences on the academic library that are likely to have a profound and permanent impact from those that are cyclical and constant in their change. Funding flows and ebbs. Scholars, students, and workers change in attitudes, interests, and characteristics. What seems most influential in our lifetime is technological development.

Technology contributes to the information problems and can be harnessed to provide solutions. The principal problems may well be information overload and the ever-growing difficulty of managing that mass; or, paradoxically, information control and the need to ensure scholarly access. The solutions lie in part in adjusting to productive use of technology, through sharper focus and greater integration of information-handling functions, through library research and action, and through expansion of the roles of academic library staff.

References

American Libraries, 1981, *12* (11), 659.

Association of Research Libraries. *ARL Statistics, 1980–81.* Washington, D.C.: Association of Research Libraries, 1981.

Battin, P. "The Real World—Large Library Organizations." Paper presented at the annual conference of the Association of American Library Schools, Denver, January 22, 1982.

Birdsall, W. F. "Librarianship, Professionalism, & Social Change." *Library Journal,* 1982, *107* (3), 223-226.

Freeman, R. B. "The Work Force of the Future: An Overview." In C. Kerr and J. M. Rosow (Eds.), *Work in America: The Decade Ahead.* New York: Van Nostrand Reinhold, 1979.

Fretwell, G. "The Association of Research Libraries' 1981 *Annual Salary Survey:* A Special Report on Rank, Salary, and Other Data." Unpublished paper, April 22, 1982.

Haas, W. J. "Professional Education and Training: A New CLR Program." Remarks presented at the 97th meeting of the Association of Research Libraries, Arlington, Va., October 16, 1980.

Isaacson, D. "Anti-Intellectualism in American Libraries." *Library Journal,* 1982, *107* (3), 227-232.

Leonard, W. P. "Desk Set II." *Journal of Academic Librarianship,* 1982, *8* (2), 95, 128.

Martin, M. S. *Issues in Personnel Management in Academic Libraries.* Greenwich, Conn.' JAI Press, 1981.

Otto, T. M. "The Academic Librarian of the 21st Century: Public Service and Library Education in the Year 2000." *Journal of Academic Librarianship,* 1982, *8* (2), 85-88.

Porat, M. U. "The Information Economy." Unpublished doctoral dissertation, Stanford University, 1976. (Facsimile reprint. Ann Arbor, Mich.: University Microfilms International, 1982.)

Smith, E. "Research Library Staffing Needs in the 1990s." Unpublished paper, January 22, 1982.

Veaner, A. B. *A Ship in Harbor Is Safe.* Westport, Conn.: Meckler Publishing, 1982.

Yankelovich, D. "Work, Values, and the New Breed." In C. Kerr and J. M. Rosow (Eds.), *Work in America: The Decade Ahead.* New York: Van Nostrand Reinhold, 1979.

Millicent D. Abell is university librarian and Jacqueline M. Coolman is personnel librarian, University of California, San Diego.

*The final step in the evolution of the college library occurs
when the library is no longer viewed as a place but as a service
in the scholarly process.*

Books, Libraries, Scholarship, and the Future

Robert A. Plane

Books and libraries have become strong popular symbols of scholarship and education. As a consequence, there is broad support for maintaining them, and loud outcries against any suggestions of change. Yet change is occurring and more will occur. If such change is understood and sensibly utilized, it can be totally constructive and can further the processes and scholarship and education.

Much is being written about the revolutionary developments of the information age in the technological library. But what we are seeing is not the start of a new revolution but the further development of one that has been raging for some 8,000 years. During that time, the world has witnessed the revolution of scholarship. And if the past is any guide to the future, the next few decades will see not the completion of this process, but instead only one more stage in its evolution.

Evolution of Scholarship

Scholarship began when humans first recorded their thoughts in pictures. A cave painting depicting a hunt made it possible for one person to

T. Galvin, B. Lynch (Eds.). *New Directions for Higher Education: Priorities for Academic Libraries*, no. 39.
San Francisco: Jossey-Bass, September 1982.

study another's perceptions of the physical world. Pictures, of course, evolved into written language, and it thus became possible to study another's thoughts and beliefs. As with any major change, there were advantages and disadvantages, benefits and costs. One of the costs was the loss of the oral tradition. There is no way we can estimate the extent of this loss. It is not surprising that history records an unbalanced account of the triumph of written communications over spoken ones. Who knows what would be the true state of today's society if it had always depended and continued to depend only on the oral tradition? Certainly it would be a different society; different in small ways and perhaps in critically large ways. Who can guess what would be the state of drama and the other arts within a totally oral tradition? Might it be possible that wisdom is more effectively communicated orally than in writing? Could we have avoided a succession of world wars?

These questions, of course, can't be answered; on the other hand, we can describe the benefits that came with written communications. Writing meant that scholarship was made possible because the bounds of distance and time were broken. Writing has made possible the recording of present events for future generations and the communication of these records throughout the world. Through writing, scholars have been able to build on the past and to interact with colleagues at great distances in order to build a worldwide body of knowledge with a great potential for benefiting all of humankind.

Somewhere in the growth of worldwide scholarship, an educated elite developed. An unforeseen cost of writing was the loss of the egalitarianism more characteristic of the oral transmission of knowledge. However, this inequity was largely overcome some 500 years ago with the invention of printing. Printing made possible wide access to written works and led to universal education so that the writings could be read by many. Those who were previously out of touch with expensive and closely held manuscripts now had access. All could learn. Universal education meant a great new supply of scholars and a more rapid generation of documents than had been imagined. It is this generation of more and more information by more and more authors that is causing the so-called crisis of information. When scholarship was confined to the few because of its dependence upon handwritten documents, there was no danger of information overflowing its bounds. But affordable printing and cheap paper made possible universal education, dispersal of useful information, and the other attractions of widespread knowledge.

The more serious cost of these developments is the problem being faced by current libraries. The problem can be summarized by noting that information is increasing at exponential rates. This means the rate at which information doubles is alarmingly fast. Depending upon the field of knowledge in question, doubling times run from as long as twenty years to as short a period as three years. If we pick ten years as an average doubling time, it follows that during the next ten years more information will be generated than in all of the

8,000 years that humans have been writing. Where we keep it all? How will we ever find it again?

Our only change to avoid being buried in paper is through utilization of computer technology. The modern computer became a possibility with the introduction of vacuum tubes into the mechanical computers of fifty years ago. Even greater possibilities emerged when the invention of the transister led to microprocessors that, during the past decade, have decreased the cost of computers while simultaneously increasing their power almost beyond belief. The introduction of such technology can and will contribute to the continuation of the revolution of scholarship. Increasingly, computer technology will aid the scholarship revolution in some spectacular ways.

Very soon it will be possible to store virtually all the information society can generate. The miniaturization made possible by microelectronics means that storage space for information has become virtually unlimited and will soon be completely affordable. Perhaps even more spectacular is the fact that it will be possible to find the information as it is needed. In other words, it can be indexed, cross-indexed, and located by microprocessors.

A bit of reflection shows, however, that these possibilities are not total blessings. As with all other major developments during the evolution of scholarship, there is a negative side: information can now be maintained without any discretionary judgment being shown. It seems likely that it is only a matter of time until the nearly infinite amount of information that is stored and indexed is totally useless. One will be able to find comprehensive documentation on both sides of every question that can possibly be posed and no doubt for some questions that cannot.

Finite library size and finite acquisition budgets forced selections to be made about which information to preserve and transmit to the next generation. It may be regrettable that, in the future, such restraints will no longer automatically operate as part of the scholarly process. However, should scholars of the future be wise enough to harness it, the same technology that made the problem can also help in its solution. Not only can the vast array of information be kept and cataloged, but it can also be ordered in regard to its usage and usefulness. There are already examples of this occurring. We are all familiar with the too widely utilized practice of counting (as opposed to reading) the publications of scholars in order to make decisions of promotion and tenure. This unfortunate practice may be changing. Through technologically generated citation indexes, it is now possible to know which publications are actually read and referred to by other scholars. Furthermore, there is the oft-quoted statistic that in a typical library 20 percent of the volumes get 80 percent of the usage. The problem always is to decide which are the 20 percent carrying the major load. Usage can now be tracked electronically, and the information gained should be useful in weeding and directing future acquisitions.

An even more significant development will be the use of information about usage in dictating the actual information generation. In other words, pubication decisions can be based on probable usage. Such developments are absolutely essential if the use of computer memory for the storing and sorting of information is going to further free scholarship from the restraint of time. Thus, if technology is cleverly and appropriately harnessed, it can keep the scholar from being totally occupied with the busy work of information retrieval. Instead, application of appropriate technology can make time available for the scholar to think about the implications of the information and thereby gain the knowledge and even the wisdom of scholarship.

The new technology can help also in freeing scholarship from the bound of distance. The new technological data base can communicate across great distances directly with other data bases. Furthermore, international communication is rapid, essentially instantaneous, so that a worldwide network of information becomes simultaneously available to scholars at every point on the face of the earth.

Distance can be further eradicated where desirable through face-to-face communication of scholars by means of video display coupled with oral transmission and, if necessary, aided by technologically assisted translation. Thus, two things are accomplished. The first is the formation of a worldwide network of scholars with common interests whose cooperative efforts are not dependent upon the accidents of geography. The second dream realized by the increased communication is the possibility of reestablishing the oral tradition. Increasingly, scholarly communication, even that involving data bases, will not have to be strained through written language. Instead, it will be more direct, through the spoken word. Because the thought process in constructing speech is different from that used to produce writing, some of the benefits that were lost with the oral tradition can be regained.

In summary, technology already available can be applied in the reasonably near future to free scholarship from the remaining bound of distance and, perhaps more importantly, the bound of time—time currently spent in travel and in the busy work of locating information. Time will then become available to scholars from the most human of all activities—human thought.

Although there will be objections, real and imagined, increased utilization of technology will be employed to aid scholarship, and most of the developments just mentioned will occur. It remains now for us to assess what this will mean for books and libraries.

The Future of Books and Libraries

The book evolved to fill a need and in the process became associated with some of the most pleasant aspects of life. As a result of its evolution, the book as we know it today is ideal for certain tasks. In computer jargon, it is "user friendly." Imagine a computer scientist describing an applied technology to a colleague by listing all its attendant advantages. The colleague becomes enthusiastic and says, "What do you call this new program?" The response, "Book." Such a scenario is indeed possible, and enthusiasm for the continuing advantages of the book is readily gained from those who have been forced to use microfilm and microfiche. Given the choice, information so stored is usually the user's last resort. However, the friendly advantages of books result from certain costs: the total economics of production, the time of production, and the need for relatively large storage space. Unlike other data bases, books are also easily stolen. Because of all these factors, books are indeed expensive, and it follows that to be published, most books must promise a large audience. A potential best-seller will often squeeze out valuable manuscripts of limited projected readership. Eventually, manuscripts with small audiences will end up in the microcomputer data base while the book format will be used for items of broad general readership.

It is predicted that although books will find less general application in the future than in the past, in some applications they will last for many years to come, certainly well into the next century. Consequently, it may be surprising to hear that libraries as such will not last as long as books. Well before the year 2000, the function of a library will have changed so drastically that it will be hard to recognize it as the same institution. The sole reason for the radical conversion will be the fact that the library will be performing services more vital to the future of scholarship. However, the transformation of the library will not occur all at once but in a series of steps.

At first, the library's job will be to use technology to make the traditional, book-based library more useful. Computers are already being extensively used to catalog, to order, and to track usage of books. Thus, libraries are able to better serve as depositories for books required by the constituents of the library.

The next step in transforming the role of libraries will be the incorporation of other technologies in order to provide wider services. A good example will be the video disk, which will store tremendous amounts of information at moderate cost. Almost all libraries at present have microfiche information storage. This none-too-popular technology will soon give way to microelectronic information storage, and the texts of whole collections will be stored on a few disks.

The next step in the evolution is also starting: the distribution of information. Library materials are made available to users who need not be present to sample holdings through on-line catalogs. Through remote terminals, users can have access to the library's list of holdings by title, author, or subject. Soon abstracts or tables of contents will be available on request at external terminal locations. Not only will the user be able to reach into the library for information, but the library will also be able to reach out for its information. Data bases at external locations can be tapped through satellite communications. In the future these two outreach functions will expand greatly, and the library will offer a worldwide store of information to users who never enter the library. Thus, the picture of a library as a place for corraling information is changed drastically. The library becomes more a switching service or a contact for serving user needs. It is at this point that the college library will at last be appreciated for what it really is and what it can offer: an educational resource in the truest sense.

Most college libraries at present are large study halls where students spend their time with information brought in from outside. This function can easily be dispersed to unused classrooms or to student dormitory rooms (made quiet through the introduction of headphones for the stereo sets). Then, overcrowded study space in libraries no longer is a pressing problem. Instead, as in the Schuler Educational Resources Center at Clarkson College, the common space can be used for personal contact between teacher and student, that is, between colleagues. It can become a place where a reintroduction of the oral tradition becomes reality.

The final step in the evolution of the college library occurs when the library is no longer viewed as a *place,* but instead as a *service* in the scholarly process. What other service is more valuable than linking together scholars without regard to time or distance, bringing together today's student with yesterday's teacher, bringing together today's scientists with their counterparts halfway around the world, bringing the leading authority to those with the greatest need to learn? As these vital services are filled increasingly by the library, the place will disappear into the central fabric of the university and become indistinguishable from the academy. And this, after all, is the image that society has always had of the library. At last the image can be reality.

The Transformed Role of the College Library

The principal change associated with this final step in the transformation of the college library is the change from a passive to an active educational role. In the first place, it will become the responsibility of library personnel to instruct students and faculty alike in the use of the services provided. In some cases where new technologies are employed, the necessary instruction will be rather extensive. However, after mastering the requisite procedures, the scholar now has access to all of the sources of information ever recorded by all the scholars who ever lived. From this point on, there is no longer a question of "Who is the teacher?" All that matters is that one is learning, and it is learning that is facilitated by the library of the future. Here one can learn about anything and learn it from the best source available, from the source chosen by the learner as being most appropriate.

Under the conditions made possible by the library of the future, two critically important jobs will emerge that the library, as an institution, will have to fill. The first of these, noted earlier, is selecting and indexing or cataloging material in order that the most useful is readily available. This is the job of the true scholar and will demand the best minds available. Technology will be able to assist in a variety of ways, from tracking usage to making cross-correlations and checking for inconsistencies. But ultimately judgment will have to be exercised, and the human mind of the librarian-scholar will play that role.

The other new role for librarians of the future will arise from the continuing progression of scholarship at an ever-accelerated rate. As it does so, various disciplines will become increasingly specialized, will rely upon more technical vocabularies, and will develop diverse methods of handling and studying information. In other words, both the vocabularies and the modes of thought will vary from discipline to discipline. Society cannot progress with a series of specialists who cannot understand each other. There will need to be communicators between disciplines, people who are conversant with more than a single discipline. The need will be met by a new group of professionals somewhat analogous to translators of foreign languages. This profession will produce secondary literatures similar to *Scientific American,* but more extensive and more specialized, probably bridging not just one discipline to the lay reader but extending one discipline to a number of specializations. Eventurally, as existing disciplines subdivide or splinter, and as each digs deeper, the job of these liaisons and their secondary literatures will grow extremely rapidly. Because each discipline is linked to a number of others, with time the secondary literature, as a function of the number of disciplines, will expand exponentially. Consequently, among the most demanded specialists in the scholarly society of the future will be the people who facilitate communication between disciplines and the scholars who judge the value of new works; these two new occupations are within the realm of the library of the future.

Predictions are always dangerous, and these predictions are dependent upon external developments having little to do with libraries or even with the university. In the first place, these predictions depend on an assumption of the supremacy of scholarship. However, recorded history shows that through many past trials, scholarship has always won. The oral tradition gave way to writing; mechanical printing and cheap paper converted growing numbers of our race into publishing scholars. The human need to learn will inevitably harness new technologies in its quest.

But there are dangers that could divert the onrush of scholarship. These include, first of all, war, which could destroy all human aspirations in a terrible instant. Another danger is that created by reemergence of the Luddites, or antitechnologists, who cast technology not as the solution to the problems caused by universal scholarship and other universal freedoms, but instead as the cause of the apparent problems. If the Luddites are successful, technology will be kept from the majority and a minority will use it to do its bidding.

However, the greatest threat would arise from a triumph of the hedonists who believe that technology should be applied solely to provide creature pleasure. They will argue: If technology is not needed to provide for the survival of the human race, it can well be used to provide instant, mindless pleasure for all. The present popularity of television is an indication of the persuasive power of this threat. It contrasts sharply with the subtler pleasures of scholarship, which demands hard work and dedication. It is my hope and belief, though, that in the end the true humanist rather than the hedonist will win. If the past is any indication, humans do ultimately value the development of ideas above the transient satisfaction of creature comforts. This humanist spirit will be satisfied by the application of technology to master time and make it available for the continuing revolution of scholarship.

Robert A. Plane is president of Clarkson College of Technology.

The editors review key points presented in this volume.

Concluding Statement

Thomas J. Galvin
Beverly P. Lynch

Libraries are integral parts of the colleges and universities they serve. Often used as indicators of institutional quality, libraries offer support to the instructional, research, and service programs that shape the academic endeavor. Academic libraries are evaluated on the number and quality of their subject collections, the quality and reliability of their reference and bibliographic services, and the competence of the staff. The alertness of the library's management, the excellence of the library's operational performance, and the adequacy of the library's physical facilities serve as other indicators of quality.

The library reflects in many ways the institution of which it is a part. Like the college or university it serves, it has become increasingly complex. The complexity of the library's operations has led to extraordinary changes in academic libraries during the past thirty years. The library, adapting in a responsive way to its environment, has handled these changes by means of the small, routine decisions that govern its daily affairs. The changes have not occured in sudden, grand decisions or in a single, vast design.

Libraries are more complex than teaching departments. Libraries serve a much larger segment of the faculty and student body. They command a much larger portion of the institution's budget. They need many more non-academic support employees. A poorly managed teaching department can be

T. Galvin, B. Lynch (Eds.). *New Directions for Higher Education: Priorities for Academic Libraries*, no. 39.
San Francisco: Jossey-Bass, September 1982.

an embarrassment; a poorly run library has an impact on the entire academic program.

To the credit of library directors, most academic libraries are well managed. Personnel policies and staff development programs, now commonplace in colleges and universities, often were implemented first in the library. Each academic library seeks to define the work of the professional and nonprofessional staff. There is constant striving to make routine the librarian's task. Jobs formerly performed by librarians now are performed by paraprofessionals, clerical help, and in some libraries, by students. While it makes choices about its present jobs and the skills required for them, the library creates new jobs requiring new skills.

Each college and university decides on the role and the status of its academic librarians. The degree of professionalism among the librarians, the quality of the research and writing they do, and the nature of the work performed by the civil service or support staff influence greatly the position of the librarians on the campus.

The role of the library director within the institution sometimes is ambiguous. He or she must identify with the faculty yet manage one of the largest budgets on the campus and one of the most complex operations. Some library directors hold the rank of dean or the title of provost in recognition of the nature of the job they hold and the expectations of the director's scholarly attainments and professional leadership.

Management information systems are in place in most libraries, designed originally to aid in the allocation of monies for library books, journals, and other materials in a rational manner among competing disciplines. Physical plant requirements shape many of the daily operational functions of libraries. Systematic review of new developments in office equipment, word-processing systems, and library automation is an on-going activity in most libraries.

The expansion of operating budgets, the demands for capital monies, and the complexity of personnel matters bring the library to the attention of campus administrators. Issues relating to the size and scope of the library's collections and the monies to maintain the collections remain high priorities within the context of the campus research programs, instructional needs, and financial resources.

The national problems related to libraries are generally agreed upon: continued exponential growth in recorded literature and information; cost pressures related to inflation, rates of exchange, and college and university budgets; emergence of new and expensive information services; the deterioration of paper; and the self-destruction of stock in many libraries are among them. Remote from the day-to-day affairs of the campus and often subtle in their complexity, the implementation of national systems of bibliographic access and control and the preservation of library materials will require institutional responses in the context of public policy.

The match or the fit between the library's goals and objectives and the goals and objectives of the college or university it serves will shape the library's overall effectiveness. The interests and requirements of the primary clientele and the library's response will determine the effectiveness.

Thomas J. Galvin is dean of the School of Library and Information Science, University of Pittsburgh.

Beverly P. Lynch is university librarian, University of Illinois at Chicago.

Sources of additional assistance are provided.

Additional Readings

Karen S. Seibert

Books

Kent, A., and others. *Use of Library Materials.* New York: Dekker, 1979.

Lancaster, F. W. *Toward Paperless Information Systems.* New York: Academic Press, 1978.

Metcalf, K. D. *Planning Academic and Research Library Buildings.* New York: McGraw-Hill, 1965.

Stueart, R. D., and Miller, G. B., Jr. (Eds.). *Collection Development in Libraries.* Greenwich, Conn.: JAI Press, 1980.

Journals

College & Research Libraries. Chicago: American Librarian Association. (Published since 1939)

Journal of Academic Librarianship. (Published since 1975)

Library Trends. Urbana: University of Illinois Press.
See specific issues:
April 1977, Vol. 25, "Trends in the Scholarly Use of Library Resources"
Fall 1977, Vol. 26, "Trends in the Governance of Libraries"
Summer 1979, Vol. 28, "The Economics of Academic Libraries"
Winter 1980, Vol 28, "Library Consultants"

T. Galvin, B. Lynch (Eds.). *New Directions for Higher Education: Priorities for Academic Libraries,* no. 39. San Francisco: Jossey-Bass, September 1982.

Yearbooks

ALA Yearbook. Chicago: American Library Association.
Advances in Librarianship. New York: Academic Press.
Annual Review of Information Science and Technology. New York: Knowledge Industry Publications.

Statistics: Annual Reports

ACRL Statistics. Chicago: American Library Association, Association of College and Research Libraries.
ARL Statistics. Washington, D.C.: Association of Research Libraries.
Library Statistics of Colleges and Universities: Institutional Data. Washington, D.C.: National Center for Education Statistics.

Karen S. Seibert is associate university librarian for public services, University of North Carolina, Chapel Hill.

Index